most loved recipe collection

P9-BUI-444

most loved

barbecuing

Pictured on Front Cover:
Top: Teriyaki Ribs, page 66
Bottom: Vegetable Skewers With
Pesto Dressing, page 105

Pictured on Back Cover:
Top Right: Chocolate Pizza, page 118
Bottom Left: Grilled Cake And Strawberries,
page 116

Most Loved Barbecuing
Copyright © Company's Coming Publishing Limited

First Printing April 2005

National Library of Canada Cataloguing in Publication

Paré, Jean
    Most loved barbecuing / Jean Paré.

(Most loved recipe collection)
Includes index.
ISBN 1-896891-65-9

    1. Barbecue cookery. I. Title. II. Series: Paré, Jean. Most loved recipe collection.

TX840.B3P39 2004   641.5'784   C2004-904528-8

Published by
Company's Coming Publishing Limited
2311 – 96 Street
Edmonton, Alberta, Canada T6N 1G3
Tel: 780-450-6223   Fax: 780-450-1857
www.companyscoming.com

Company's Coming is a registered trademark owned by
Company's Coming Publishing Limited

Printed in China

We gratefully acknowledge the following suppliers for their generous support of our Test Kitchen and Photo Studio:

Broil King Barbecues
Corelle ®
Hamilton Beach ® Canada
Lagostina ®
Proctor Silex ® Canada
Tupperware ®

Our special thanks to the following businesses for providing extensive props for photography:

Anchor Hocking Canada
Barbecue Country
Bissett Stained Glass
Browne & Co.
Canhome Global
Casa Bugatti
Cherison Enterprises Inc.
Danesco Inc.
Dansk Gifts
Klass Works
Linens 'N Things
Mikasa Home Store
Out of the Fire Studio
Pfaltzgraff Canada
Pier 1 Imports
Pyrex® Storage
Sears Canada
Soulminder Steel & Art Studio
Stokes
The Bay
The Paderno Factory Store
Winners Stores

Pictured from left: Balsamic Peaches, page 114; Super Oz Burgers, page 46; Quick Corn, page 102; Barbecued Shrimp, page 14.

table of contents

the Company's Coming story

"never share a recipe you wouldn't use yourself"

Jean Paré grew up understanding that the combination of family, friends and home cooking is the essence of a good life. From her mother she learned to appreciate good cooking, while her father praised even her earliest attempts. When she left home she took with her many acquired family recipes, a love of cooking and an intriguing desire to read recipe books like novels!

In 1963, when her four children had all reached school age, Jean volunteered to cater the 50th anniversary of the Vermilion School of Agriculture, now Lakeland College. Working out of her home, Jean prepared a dinner for over 1000 people which launched a flourishing catering operation that continued for over eighteen years. During that time she was provided with countless opportunities to test new ideas with immediate feedback—resulting in empty plates and contented customers! Whether preparing cocktail sandwiches for a house party or serving a hot meal for 1500 people, Jean Paré earned a reputation for good food, courteous service and reasonable prices.

"Why don't you write a cookbook?" Time and again, as requests for her recipes mounted, Jean was asked that question. Jean's response was to team up with her son, Grant Lovig, in the fall of 1980 to form Company's Coming Publishing Limited. April 14, 1981 marked the debut of "150 DELICIOUS SQUARES," the first Company's Coming cookbook in what soon would become Canada's most popular cookbook series.

Jean Paré's operation has grown steadily from the early days of working out of a spare bedroom in her home. Full-time staff includes marketing personnel located in major cities across Canada. Home Office is based in Edmonton, Alberta in a modern building constructed specially for the company.

Today the company distributes throughout Canada and the United States in addition to numerous overseas markets, all under the guidance of Jean's daughter, Gail Lovig. Best-sellers many times over in English, Company's Coming cookbooks have also been published in French and Spanish. Familiar and trusted in home kitchens around the world, Company's Coming cookbooks are offered in a variety of formats, including the original softcover series.

Jean Paré's approach to cooking has always called for quick and easy recipes using everyday ingredients. Even when travelling, she is constantly on the lookout for new ideas to share with her readers. At home, she can usually be found researching and writing recipes, or working in the company's test kitchen. Jean continues to gain new supporters by adhering to what she calls "the golden rule of cooking:" never share a recipe you wouldn't use yourself. It's an approach that works—*millions of times over!*

foreword

You'll never be at a loss for something delicious to grill with *Most Loved Barbecuing*. Leaf through pages of time-tested, beautifully photographed, consistently delicious recipes that use ingredients you already have on hand.

Though we can barbecue year-round, with the approach of summer, we rush to our outdoor grills for the great taste of something smoked and sizzling. Barbecuing isn't only for steaks, burgers or potatoes—though sometimes nothing could be better! It's also for baking muffins, cakes or bread, grilling vegetables or fruit, or cooking roasts and ribs. You can prepare appetizers, side dishes, entrées and desserts using this one versatile appliance, without all those extra pots and pans to clean later. For even easier cleanup, use foil and foil pans.

When you barbecue, it feels less like work and more like taking the time to grill a meal you'll enjoy with your family and friends. And because you aren't stuck in the kitchen, you can join the party while grilling something tantalizing.

Don't forget to add extra flavour to your meat with a spicy rub or marinade, or complement your meal with a delicious sauce or dip, crisp salad, fresh vegetables or fruit. The contrast between the hot food coming off the barbecue and the cool food from the refrigerator will please your palate. Be close by when the cook calls because you won't want to miss a bite!

We've included recipes that use direct and indirect cooking methods. For indirect cooking, the burner under the food is turned off and the opposite burner is left on. The lid is always closed to maintain an even heat for cooking such foods as pies, cakes, bread, Yorkshire pudding, meat and poultry. We've also compiled helpful hints to ensure your barbecuing success. All recipes have been tested on a gas barbecue.

Whether it's vegetables or fruit, breads or buns, fish or poultry, beef or pork, *Most Loved Barbecuing* helps you grill it to perfection. So, get out of the kitchen and into the great outdoors. It's a perfect time to put some sizzle into all your favourite meals!

Jean Paré

nutrition information guidelines

Each recipe is analyzed using the most current version of the Canadian Nutrient File from Health Canada, which is based on the United States Department of Agriculture (USDA) Nutrient Database.

- If more than one ingredient is listed (such as "hard margarine or butter"), or if a range is given (1 – 2 tsp., 5 – 10 mL), only the first ingredient or first amount is analyzed.

- For meat, poultry and fish, the serving size per person is based on the recommended 4 oz. (113 g) uncooked weight (without bone), which is 2 – 3 oz. (57 – 85 g) cooked weight (without bone)— approximately the size of a deck of playing cards.

- Milk used is 1% M.F. (milk fat), unless otherwise stated.

- Cooking oil used is canola oil, unless otherwise stated.

- Ingredients indicating "sprinkle," "optional," or "for garnish" are not included in the nutrition information.

Margaret Ng, B.Sc. (Hon), M.A.
Registered Dietitian

Red wine and mustard are classic marinade partners, especially when teamed with garlic and pepper, as in this recipe.

Red Wine, Mustard And Garlic Marinade

Dry red (or alcohol-free) wine	1 cup	250 mL
Dijon mustard (with whole seeds)	2 tbsp.	30 mL
Barbecue sauce (your favourite)	2 tbsp.	30 mL
Worcestershire sauce	1 tbsp.	15 mL
Olive (or cooking) oil	1 tbsp.	15 mL
Garlic cloves, minced (or 1 tsp., 5 mL, powder)	4	4
Pepper	1 tsp.	5 mL

Combine all 7 ingredients in small bowl. Makes about 1 1/3 cups (325 mL).

1 tbsp. (15 mL): 17 Calories; 0.7 g Total Fat (0.5 g Mono, 0.1 g Poly, 0.1 g Sat); 0 mg Cholesterol; 1 g Carbohydrate; trace Fibre; 0 g Protein; 39 mg Sodium

Pictured on page 7.

This combination of lively spices is tempered nicely by the addition of fresh herbs.

Spice And Herb Marinade

Orange juice	1/2 cup	125 mL
Dry white (or alcohol-free) wine	1/2 cup	125 mL
Chopped fresh cilantro or parsley (or 1 tbsp., 15 mL, dried)	1/4 cup	60 mL
Chopped fresh mint leaves (or 1 tbsp., 15 mL, dried)	1/4 cup	60 mL
Olive (or cooking) oil	2 tbsp.	30 mL
Liquid honey	2 tbsp.	30 mL
Garlic cloves, minced (or 1/2 tsp., 2 mL, powder)	2	2
Grated orange zest	1 tsp.	5 mL
Ground cumin	1 tsp.	5 mL
Ground cinnamon	1/2 tsp.	2 mL
Ground ginger	1/2 tsp.	2 mL
Chili powder	1/4 tsp.	1 mL

Combine all 12 ingredients in small bowl. Makes about 1 1/3 cups (325 mL).

1 tbsp. (15 mL): 25 Calories; 1.3 g Total Fat (0.9 g Mono, 0.1 g Poly, 0.2 g Sat); 0 mg Cholesterol; 3 g Carbohydrate; trace Fibre; 0 g Protein; 1 mg Sodium

Pictured on page 7.

Top Right: Spice And Herb Marinade, above
Bottom Left: Red Wine, Mustard And Garlic
Marinade, this page

Look no further for the world's greatest steak sauce. Mildly spiced and creamy. Perfect for a juicy grilled T-bone or porterhouse steak.

Green Peppercorn Sauce

Hard margarine (or butter)	1 tbsp.	15 mL
Small onion, finely chopped	1	1
Garlic cloves, minced (or 1/2 tsp., 2 mL, powder)	2	2
Brandy	2 tbsp.	30 mL
Whipping cream	1 1/2 cups	375 mL
Can of green peppercorns in brine, drained	1 oz.	30 g
Prepared mustard	1 tsp.	5 mL
Salt	1/4 tsp.	1 mL

Melt margarine in large frying pan on medium. Add onion. Cook for 5 to 10 minutes, stirring often, until softened.

Add garlic. Heat and stir for 1 to 2 minutes until fragrant. Add brandy. Immediately ignite with match to burn off alcohol.

Add remaining 4 ingredients. Heat and stir for 5 to 10 minutes until boiling and slightly thickened. Makes about 1 1/2 cups (375 mL).

1 tbsp. (15 mL): 54 Calories; 5.3 g Total Fat (1.7 g Mono, 0.2 g Poly, 3.1 g Sat); 18 mg Cholesterol; 1 g Carbohydrate; trace Fibre; 0 g Protein; 38 mg Sodium

Pictured on page 9.

A mild marinade. Great for shrimp or other seafood.

Lemon Marinade

Cooking oil	1/2 cup	125 mL
Juice and sliced peel of small lemon	1	1
Dried thyme	1/2 tsp.	2 mL
Garlic powder	1/4 tsp.	1 mL
Seasoned salt	1/4 tsp.	1 mL
Salt	1/4 tsp.	1 mL
Pepper, sprinkle		
Hot pepper sauce (optional)	1/8 tsp.	0.5 mL

Combine all 8 ingredients in small bowl. Makes about 3/4 cup (175 mL).

1 tbsp. (15 mL): 84 Calories; 9.2 g Total Fat (5.4 g Mono, 2.7 g Poly, 0.7 g Sat); 0 mg Cholesterol; 1 g Carbohydrate; trace Fibre; 0 g Protein; 72 mg Sodium

Pictured on page 9.

Left: Green Peppercorn Sauce, this page
Right: Lemon Marinade, above

Plan an Indian-style barbecue using this basting sauce to add great flavour to beef. Use a hotter curry paste if you prefer more spice.

Curried Yogurt Basting Sauce

Plain yogurt	1 1/4 cups	300 mL
Curry paste	1/4 cup	60 mL
Chopped fresh mint leaves (or 1 tbsp., 15 mL, dried)	1/4 cup	60 mL
Chopped fresh cilantro or parsley (or 1 tbsp., 15 mL, dried)	1/4 cup	60 mL
Mango chutney	2 tbsp.	30 mL

Combine all 5 ingredients in medium bowl. Makes about 1 1/2 cups (375 mL).

1 tbsp. (15 mL): 21 Calories; 1.4 g Total Fat (0.7 g Mono, 0.3 g Poly, 0.2 g Sat); 1 mg Cholesterol; 2 g Carbohydrate; trace Fibre; 1 g Protein; 10 mg Sodium

Pictured on page 11.

A versatile sauce—tastes great with beef, chicken, fish or pork.

Fast Teriyaki Sauce

Soy sauce	1/2 cup	125 mL
Cooking oil	1/4 cup	60 mL
Ketchup	1 tbsp.	15 mL
Garlic powder	1/4 tsp.	1 mL

Combine all 4 ingredients in small bowl. Makes about 3/4 cup (175 mL).

1 tbsp. (15 mL): 50 Calories; 4.6 g Total Fat (2.7 g Mono, 1.4 g Poly, 0.3 g Sat); 0 mg Cholesterol; 1 g Carbohydrate; trace Fibre; 1 g Protein; 709 mg Sodium

Pictured on page 11.

Top Right: Curried Yogurt Basting Sauce, this page
Bottom Left: Fast Teriyaki Sauce, above

Herbs and spice are always nice. Give them a shake — try them rubbed on steak.

Steak Rubs

LEMON PEPPER RUB

Garlic powder	1 tsp.	5 mL
Lemon pepper	1 tsp.	5 mL
Grated lemon zest	1/2 tsp.	2 mL
Dried basil	1/2 tsp.	2 mL

Combine all 4 ingredients in small cup. Makes about 1 tbsp. (15 mL).

1/2 tsp. (2 mL): 2 Calories; 0 g Total Fat (0 g Mono, 0 g Poly, 0 g Sat); 0 mg Cholesterol; 1 g Carbohydrate; trace Fibre; 0 g Protein; 198 mg Sodium

Pictured on page 13.

HERB AND SPICE RUB

Parsley flakes, crushed	1 tbsp.	15 mL
Paprika	1 tsp.	5 mL
Garlic powder	1 tsp.	5 mL
Pepper	1/4 tsp.	1 mL

Combine all 4 ingredients in small cup. Makes about 1 1/2 tbsp. (25 mL).

1/2 tsp. (2 mL): 2 Calories; 0 g Total Fat (0 g Mono, 0 g Poly, 0 g Sat); 0 mg Cholesterol; 0 g Carbohydrate; trace Fibre; 0 g Protein; 1 mg Sodium

Pictured on page 13.

CHILI RUB

Onion powder	1 tsp.	5 mL
Chili powder	1 tsp.	5 mL
Garlic salt	1 tsp.	5 mL
Dried whole oregano, crushed	1 tsp.	5 mL
Ground cumin	1 tsp.	5 mL

Combine all 5 ingredients in small cup. Makes about 1 1/2 tbsp. (25 mL).

1/2 tsp. (2 mL): 4 Calories; 0.1 g Total Fat (0 g Mono, 0 g Poly, 0 g Sat); 0 mg Cholesterol; 1 g Carbohydrate; trace Fibre; 0 g Protein; 135 mg Sodium

Pictured on page 13.

(continued on next page)

NEW ORLEANS RUB

Garlic salt	1 tsp.	5 mL
Curry powder	1 tsp.	5 mL
Paprika	1 tsp.	5 mL
Cayenne pepper	1/4 tsp.	1 mL

Combine all 4 ingredients in small cup. Makes about 1 tbsp. (15 mL).

1/2 tsp. (2 mL): 3 Calories; 0.1 g Total Fat (0 g Mono, 0 g Poly, 0 g Sat); 0 mg Cholesterol; 1 g Carbohydrate; trace Fibre; 0 g Protein; 198 mg Sodium

Pictured below.

Top Left: Lemon Pepper Rub, page 12
Top Right: Chili Rub, page 12
Bottom Left: Herb And Spice Rub, page 12
Bottom Right: New Orleans Rub, this page

Perfectly marinated and barbecued shrimp served with a rich garlic mayonnaise.

Barbecued Shrimp

GARLIC MAYONNAISE

Large egg	1	1
Egg yolk (large)	1	1
Lemon juice	1 tbsp.	15 mL
Garlic clove, minced (or 1/4 tsp., 1 mL, powder)	1	1
Salt	1/8 tsp.	0.5 mL
Cooking oil	3/4 cup	175 mL

SEAFOOD MARINADE

Chopped fresh parsley (or 2 1/4 tsp., 11 mL, flakes)	3 tbsp.	50 mL
Cooking oil	2 tbsp.	30 mL
Grated lemon zest	1/2 tsp.	2 mL
Salt	1/2 tsp.	2 mL
Pepper	1/2 tsp.	2 mL
Fresh uncooked jumbo shrimp (tails intact), peeled and deveined	18	18

Garlic Mayonnaise: Process first 5 ingredients in blender or food processor for about 2 minutes until creamy.

With motor running, slowly pour first amount of cooking oil through hole in lid until mixture is pale and thickened. Transfer to small bowl. Cover with plastic wrap. Chill for at least 1 hour to blend flavours. Makes about 1 cup (250 mL) mayonnaise.

Seafood Marinade: Combine next 5 ingredients in medium bowl. Makes about 1/3 cup (75 mL) marinade.

Add shrimp. Toss until coated. Cover with plastic wrap. Marinate in refrigerator for at least 1 hour, stirring occasionally. Drain and discard marinade. Preheat barbecue to medium. Cook shrimp on greased grill for about 5 minutes, turning occasionally, until shrimp are pink. Do not overcook. Serve with Garlic Mayonnaise. Serves 6.

1 serving: 364 Calories; 33.9 g Total Fat (19.2 g Mono, 9.9 g Poly, 2.9 g Sat); 163 mg Cholesterol; 1 g Carbohydrate; trace Fibre; 14 g Protein; 251 mg Sodium

Pictured on page 15.

Bulgogi (bul-GO-gee) is a popular Korean beef dish. Makes a great appetizer for a summer patio party.

Bulgogi Vegetable Bundles

BULGOGI MARINADE

Indonesian sweet (or thick) soy sauce	1/4 cup	60 mL
Water	1/4 cup	60 mL
Cooking oil	1 tbsp.	15 mL
Dry sherry	1 tbsp.	15 mL
Garlic cloves, minced (or 1/2 tsp., 2 mL, powder)	2	2
Green onion, cut into 4 pieces	1	1
Sesame seeds, toasted (see Note)	2 tsp.	10 mL
Flank steak, cut diagonally into 1/8 inch (3 mm) thick slices (see Note)	3/4 lb.	340 g
Steamed whole carrots, cut into 4 inch (10 cm) lengths, quartered lengthwise	4	4
Steamed fresh asparagus (or whole green beans), cut into 4 inch (10 cm) lengths	10	10
Roasted red peppers, cut into 4 inch (10 cm) strips	2	2
Lightly steamed medium zucchini (with peel), cut lengthwise into 8 pieces, then into 4 inch (10 cm) lengths	1	1
Bamboo skewers (8 inch, 20 cm, length), soaked in water for 10 minutes	20	20

Bulgogi Marinade: Process first 7 ingredients in blender or food processor until smooth. Makes about 3/4 cup (175 mL) marinade. Pour into large resealable freezer bag.

Add steak slices. Seal bag. Turn until coated. Marinate in refrigerator for at least 2 hours, turning occasionally. Drain and discard marinade.

Divide and layer vegetables crosswise on steak slices. Roll up into bundles. Thread 2 bundles onto 2 skewers, ladder-style. Preheat barbecue to medium. Cook bundles on greased grill for about 2 1/2 minutes per side until steak slices are cooked to desired doneness. Serves 10.

1 serving: 98 Calories; 4 g Total Fat (1.7 g Mono, 0.5 g Poly, 1.4 g Sat); 14 mg Cholesterol; 7 g Carbohydrate; 2 g Fibre; 9 g Protein; 199 mg Sodium

Pictured on pages 18/19.

Tandoori Pork Bites

Plain yogurt	2/3 cup	150 mL
Tandoori paste	1/2 cup	125 mL
Mango chutney	1/3 cup	75 mL
Pork tenderloin, trimmed of fat, cut into 3/4 inch (2 cm) cubes	1 lb.	454 g
Bamboo skewers (8 inch, 20 cm, length), soaked in water for 10 minutes	8	8
MANGO YOGURT DIP		
Plain yogurt	1/2 cup	125 mL
Mango chutney	1/3 cup	75 mL

The yogurt dip cools these spicy bite-size appetizers.

Combine first 3 ingredients in large bowl. Makes about 1 1/2 cups (375 mL) marinade.

Add pork. Stir until coated. Cover with plastic wrap. Marinate in refrigerator for at least 6 hours or overnight, stirring occasionally. Drain and discard marinade.

Thread 4 pork cubes onto each skewer. Preheat barbecue to medium. Cook skewers on greased grill for 5 to 7 minutes, turning occasionally, until pork is no longer pink inside.

Mango Yogurt Dip: Combine yogurt and chutney in small bowl. Makes about 1 cup (250 mL) dip. Serve with pork bites. Makes 8 skewers.

1 skewer with 2 tbsp. (30 mL) dip: 113 Calories; 1.9 g Total Fat (0.8 g Mono, 0.2 g Poly, 0.8 g Sat); 35 mg Cholesterol; 9 g Carbohydrate; trace Fibre; 15 g Protein; 197 mg Sodium

Pictured on page 18.

Photo Legend, next page

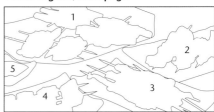

1. Bulgogi Vegetable Bundles, page 16
2. Satay, page 20
3. Korean Skewered Pork, page 21
4. Tandoori Pork Bites, this page
5. Mango Yogurt Dip, this page

Tender sirloin gently barbecued to flavourful perfection. You'll crave this.

note

To slice meat easily, place in freezer for about 30 minutes until just beginning to freeze. If using from frozen state, partially thaw before slicing.

Satay

SATAY MARINADE

Soy sauce	2/3 cup	150 mL
Granulated sugar	1/3 cup	75 mL
Ketchup	2 tbsp.	30 mL
Cooking oil	2 tbsp.	30 mL
Ground ginger	1/2 tsp.	2 mL
Garlic powder	1/4 tsp.	1 mL
Onion powder	1/4 tsp.	1 mL
Beef sirloin tip roast, thinly cut across the grain (see Note)	1 1/2 lbs.	680 g
Bamboo skewers (8 inch, 20 cm, length), soaked in water for 10 minutes	6	6

Satay Marinade: Combine first 7 ingredients in large bowl. Makes about 1 cup (250 mL) marinade.

Cut beef slices into 1 1/2 to 2 inch (3.8 to 5 cm) long strips. Add beef to marinade. Stir until coated. Cover with plastic wrap. Marinate in refrigerator for at least 30 minutes, stirring occasionally. Drain and discard marinade.

Thread beef, accordion-style, onto skewers. Preheat barbecue to medium-high. Cook skewers on greased grill for 4 to 5 minutes, turning occasionally, until desired doneness. Makes 6 skewers.

1 skewer: 218 Calories; 8.2 g Total Fat (3.9 g Mono, 1 g Poly, 2.3 g Sat); 54 mg Cholesterol; 8 g Carbohydrate; trace Fibre; 27 g Protein; 1074 mg Sodium

Pictured on page 19.

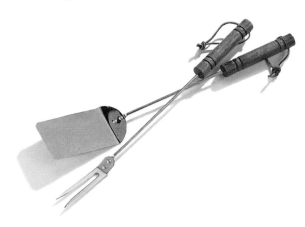

Korean Skewered Pork

SWEET CHILI MARINADE

Low-sodium soy sauce	1/3 cup	75 mL
Sweet chili sauce	1/4 cup	60 mL
Sesame oil, for flavour	1 tbsp.	15 mL
Sesame seeds, toasted (see Note)	1 tbsp.	15 mL
Garlic cloves, minced (or 1 tsp., 5 mL, powder)	4	4
Brown sugar, packed	2 tsp.	10 mL
Finely grated, peeled gingerroot (or 1/4 tsp., 1 mL, ground ginger)	1 tsp.	5 mL
Chili paste (sambal oelek)	1 tsp.	5 mL
Boneless pork shoulder butt roast, cut diagonally into 1/8 inch (3 mm) thick slices (see Note)	1 1/2 lbs.	680 g
Bamboo skewers (8 inch, 20 cm, length), soaked in water for 10 minutes	12	12

Sweet Chili Marinade: Combine first 8 ingredients in small bowl. Makes about 3/4 cup (175 mL) marinade. Pour into large resealable freezer bag.

Add pork. Seal bag. Turn until coated. Marinate in refrigerator for at least 6 hours or overnight, turning occasionally. Drain and discard marinade.

Thread pork loosely, accordion-style, onto skewers. Preheat barbecue to medium-high. Cook skewers on greased grill for 5 to 7 minutes per side until pork is no longer pink. Makes 12 skewers.

1 skewer: 152 Calories; 11.2 g Total Fat (4.9 g Mono, 1.4 g Poly, 3.7 g Sat); 34 mg Cholesterol; 2 g Carbohydrate; trace Fibre; 11 g Protein; 188 mg Sodium

Pictured on page 19.

Tasty skewers with a mild ginger and sesame flavour. For thin pork slices, ask your butcher to slice the roast with a meat cutter.

notes

To toast seeds, spread evenly in ungreased shallow pan. Bake in 350°F (175°C) oven for 5 to 10 minutes, stirring or shaking often, until desired doneness.

To slice meat easily, place in freezer for about 30 minutes until just beginning to freeze. If using from frozen state, partially thaw before slicing.

Small toasted bread rounds topped with sweet roasted peppers and feta cheese. It's bruschetta with a Greek twist.

serving suggestion

Bruschetta can also be served as a light lunch, evening snack or as part of an antipasto platter.

Red Pepper Bruschetta

Red medium pepper, quartered, seeds and ribs removed	1	1
Yellow medium pepper, quartered, seeds and ribs removed	1	1
Finely chopped fresh parsley (or 1 1/2 tsp., 7 mL, flakes)	2 tbsp.	30 mL
Finely chopped red onion	2 tbsp.	30 mL
Olive (or cooking) oil	1 tbsp.	15 mL
Red wine vinegar	2 tsp.	10 mL
Granulated sugar	1/2 tsp.	2 mL
Salt	1/4 tsp.	1 mL
Pepper, just a pinch		
Baguette bread loaf (about 24 inch, 60 cm, length), cut diagonally into 1/2 inch (12 mm) thick slices	1	1
Olive (or cooking) oil	2 tbsp.	30 mL
Garlic clove, halved	1	1
Crumbled feta cheese	1 cup	250 mL

Preheat barbecue to high. Arrange red and yellow peppers, skin-side down, on greased grill. Cook for 10 to 15 minutes until skins are blistered and blackened. Remove to medium bowl. Cover with plastic wrap. Let sweat for about 15 minutes until cool enough to handle. Peel and discard skins. Chop finely. Return to same bowl.

Add next 7 ingredients. Stir. Cover with plastic wrap. Chill for at least 1 hour, stirring occasionally, to blend flavours. Makes about 1 cup (250 mL) pepper mixture.

Reduce barbecue heat to low. Brush both sides of baguette slices with second amount of olive oil. Place slices on grill. Toast both sides until lightly browned.

Rub 1 side of each baguette slice with garlic clove. Divide and spoon pepper mixture on top.

Sprinkle feta cheese over top of pepper mixture on each slice. Makes about 30 bruschetta.

1 bruschetta: 51 Calories; 2.8 g Total Fat (1.4 g Mono, 0.2 g Poly, 1.1 g Sat); 5 mg Cholesterol; 5 g Carbohydrate; trace Fibre; 2 g Protein; 127 mg Sodium

Pictured on page 23.

Have these for a quick snack when you're in the mood for something cheesy and crispy.

serving suggestion

Serve with sour cream and salsa, along with an icy cold glass of your favourite summer punch.

variation

Place sheet of heavy-duty (or double layer of regular) foil on baking sheet. Grease foil with cooking spray. Crowd chips into 1 large circle. Cook as directed.

Pictured on page 25.

Nachos

Bag of corn (or tortilla) chips	9 oz.	240 g
Grated Monterey Jack cheese	1 1/4 cups	300 mL
Grated medium Cheddar cheese	1 1/4 cups	300 mL
Bacon slices, cooked crisp and crumbled	6	6
Can of diced green chilies	4 oz.	113 g
Green onions, sliced	3	3

Cut six 12 inch (30 cm) squares of heavy-duty (or double layer of regular) foil. Grease each square with cooking spray. Arrange chips in 6 inch (15 cm) circle on each square. Crowd chips together so little or no foil is visible through them.

Divide and layer remaining 5 ingredients, in order given, on top of chips. Preheat barbecue to medium-low. Place squares on ungreased grill. Close lid. Cook for 5 to 10 minutes until cheese is melted. Check often, as they burn easily. Serves 6.

1 serving: 335 Calories; 21.2 g Total Fat (9.9 g Mono, 2.1 g Poly, 7.9 g Sat); 28 mg Cholesterol; 27 g Carbohydrate; 3 g Fibre; 11 g Protein; 447 mg Sodium

You haven't had pizza until you've had it made on the barbecue! Add any deli meats you like for your own unique touch.

birthday pizza

Arrange strips of green or red pepper on top of pizza in the shape of the number that represents the birthday year!

Pizza On The Grill

Biscuit mix	2 cups	500 mL
Milk	1/2 cup	125 mL
Pasta (or pizza) sauce	1 cup	250 mL
Grated part-skim mozzarella cheese	2 cups	500 mL
Sliced fresh white mushrooms	1 cup	250 mL
Chopped deli meat (your favourite)	1 cup	250 mL
Chopped green onion	1/2 cup	125 mL
Chopped red pepper	1/2 cup	125 mL
Grated part-skim mozzarella cheese	1 cup	250 mL

Measure biscuit mix into medium bowl. Add milk. Stir until just moistened. Turn out dough onto lightly floured surface. Knead 8 to 10 times. Press evenly in greased 12 inch (30 cm) pizza pan. Preheat barbecue to high. Place pan on 1 side of ungreased grill. Turn off burner under pan, turning opposite burner down to medium. Close lid. Cook for about 15 minutes, rotating pan at halftime, until crust is just starting to turn golden.

Spread pasta sauce evenly over crust.

Layer next 5 ingredients, in order given, over sauce.

Sprinkle with second amount of mozzarella cheese. Return to unlit side of grill. Close lid. Cook for about 15 minutes until heated through and cheese is melted. Cuts into 6 wedges.

1 wedge: 481 Calories; 22.9 g Total Fat (8.1 g Mono, 4 g Poly, 9.3 g Sat); 57 mg Cholesterol; 41 g Carbohydrate; 1 g Fibre; 27 g Protein; 1560 mg Sodium

Pictured on page 27.

These are a welcome change from bread or dinner rolls for any barbecued meal.

dotted corn muffins

Add 3 tbsp. (50 mL) chopped green onion and 2 tbsp. (30 mL) each of chopped green pepper and red pepper to egg mixture before adding to well.

Corn Muffins

All-purpose flour	1 1/4 cups	300 mL
Yellow cornmeal	3/4 cup	175 mL
Granulated sugar	1/4 cup	60 mL
Baking powder	2 tsp.	10 mL
Salt	1/2 tsp.	2 mL
Plain yogurt	1 cup	250 mL
Cooking oil	1/4 cup	60 mL
Large egg	1	1

Measure first 5 ingredients into large bowl. Stir. Make a well in centre.

Combine remaining 3 ingredients in small bowl. Add to well. Stir until just moistened. Grease 12 muffin cups with cooking spray. Fill cups 3/4 full. Preheat barbecue to high. Place muffin pan on 1 side of ungreased grill. Turn off burner under muffin pan, turning opposite burner down to medium. Close lid. Cook for 20 to 25 minutes, rotating pan at halftime, until muffins are golden and wooden pick inserted in centre of muffin comes out clean. Let stand in pan for 5 minutes before removing to wire rack to cool. Makes 12 muffins.

1 muffin: 164 Calories; 5.9 g Total Fat (3.2 g Mono, 1.6 g Poly, 0.7 g Sat); 19 mg Cholesterol; 24 g Carbohydrate; 1 g Fibre; 4 g Protein; 182 mg Sodium

Pictured on pages 30/31.

Blueberry Muffins

A delicious treat for a barbecue brunch.

Hard margarine (or butter), softened	1/4 cup	60 mL
Granulated sugar	1/4 cup	60 mL
Large egg	1	1
All-purpose flour	1 3/4 cups	425 mL
Baking powder	4 tsp.	20 mL
Grated lemon zest	1 tsp.	5 mL
Salt	1/2 tsp.	2 mL
Milk	1 cup	250 mL
Fresh (or frozen, thawed) blueberries	1 cup	250 mL
All-purpose flour	1/4 cup	60 mL

Cream margarine and sugar in large bowl. Add egg. Beat until smooth.

Combine next 4 ingredients in medium bowl.

Add flour mixture to margarine mixture in 3 additions, alternating with milk in 2 additions, beginning and ending with flour mixture, stirring after each addition until just moistened.

Measure blueberries into small bowl. Sprinkle with second amount of flour. Toss gently until coated. Add to batter. Stir gently. Grease 12 muffin cups with cooking spray. Fill cups 3/4 full. Preheat barbecue to high. Place muffin pan on 1 side of ungreased grill. Turn off burner under muffin pan, turning opposite burner down to medium. Close lid. Cook for about 25 minutes, rotating pan at halftime, until muffins are golden and wooden pick inserted in centre of muffin comes out clean. Let stand in pan for 5 minutes before removing to wire rack to cool. Makes 12 muffins.

1 muffin: 157 Calories; 5 g Total Fat (2.9 g Mono, 0.6 g Poly, 1.1 g Sat); 19 mg Cholesterol; 25 g Carbohydrate; 1 g Fibre; 4 g Protein; 287 mg Sodium

Pictured on page 31.

Photo Legend, next page

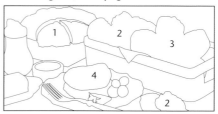

Hot biscuits are a great addition to any meal.

note

To make sour milk, measure 1 tbsp. (15 mL) white vinegar or lemon juice into 1 cup (250 mL) liquid measure. Add milk to make 3/4 cup (175 mL) liquid. Stir.

serving suggestion

An ideal side for Chicken And Artichoke Salad, page 38, or Barbecued Pork Salad, page 45.

Barbecued Biscuit

All-purpose flour	2 cups	500 mL
Baking powder	4 tsp.	20 mL
Baking soda	1/2 tsp.	2 mL
Salt	3/4 tsp.	4 mL
Hard margarine (or butter), cut up	3 tbsp.	50 mL
Sour milk (see Note)	3/4 cup	175 mL

Combine first 4 ingredients in medium bowl. Cut in margarine until mixture resembles coarse crumbs.

Add sour milk. Stir until just moistened. Turn out dough onto lightly floured surface. Knead 8 to 10 times. Flatten dough into 3/4 inch (2 cm) thick disc. Place on 1 sheet of greased heavy-duty (or double layer of regular) foil. Do not enclose. Preheat barbecue to high. Place foil with dough on 1 side of ungreased grill. Turn off burner under foil, turning opposite burner down to medium. Close lid. Cook for 15 to 18 minutes, rotating foil at halftime, until biscuit is lightly golden. Cuts into 8 wedges.

1 wedge: 170 Calories; 4.9 g Total Fat (2.9 g Mono, 0.6 g Poly, 1.1 g Sat); 1 mg Cholesterol; 27 g Carbohydrate; 1 g Fibre; 4 g Protein; 551 mg Sodium

Pictured on page 30.

Buttermilk Pancakes

All-purpose flour	2 cups	500 mL
Baking powder	2 tsp.	10 mL
Baking soda	1 tsp.	5 mL
Salt	1 tsp.	5 mL
Buttermilk (or reconstituted from powder)	2 cups	500 mL
Cooking oil	2 tbsp.	30 mL
Large eggs	2	2
Cooking oil	2 tsp.	10 mL

Measure first 4 ingredients into large bowl. Stir. Make a well in centre.

Combine next 3 ingredients in medium bowl. Add to well. Stir until just moistened. Batter will be lumpy.

Place griddle on barbecue grill. Preheat barbecue to medium. Brush 1/2 tsp. (2 mL) of second amount of cooking oil on griddle. Heat until hot. Pour about 1/4 cup (60 mL) batter onto griddle for each pancake. Cook for 2 to 3 minutes until edges of pancakes appear dry and bubbles form on top. Turn. Cook for about 2 minutes until golden. Repeat with remaining batter, brushing more cooking oil on griddle with each batch if necessary to prevent sticking. Makes 14 pancakes.

1 pancake: 118 Calories; 3.9 g Total Fat (1.9 g Mono, 1 g Poly, 0.6 g Sat); 32 mg Cholesterol; 16 g Carbohydrate; 1 g Fibre; 4 g Protein; 362 mg Sodium

Pictured on page 30.

Put the griddle on the barbecue and enjoy an outdoor brunch. Don't have a griddle? A cast-iron frying pan works just as well.

serving suggestion

Add an assortment of fresh fruit on the side for a complete breakfast.

Crispy on the outside; tender and golden on the inside. Oregano and chili accent Cheddar cheese in this delicious bread.

Chili Herb Bread

Finely grated sharp Cheddar cheese	2/3 cup	150 mL
Hard margarine (or butter), softened	2/3 cup	150 mL
Chili powder	1 tsp.	5 mL
Dried whole oregano	3/4 tsp.	4 mL
French bread loaf, cut into 1 inch (2.5 cm) thick slices	1	1

Measure first 4 ingredients into small bowl. Beat well. Makes about 1 1/4 cups (300 mL) cheese mixture.

Spread cheese mixture evenly on 1 side of each bread slice. Arrange slices into loaf shape. Place on 1 sheet of heavy-duty (or double layer of regular) foil. Fold edges of foil to enclose. Preheat barbecue to medium. Place foil with loaf on ungreased grill. Close lid. Cook for about 15 minutes, turning occasionally, until cheese is melted. Makes about 14 slices.

1 slice: 195 Calories; 12.1 g Total Fat (6.9 g Mono, 1.2 g Poly, 3.3 g Sat); 6 mg Cholesterol; 17 g Carbohydrate; 1 g Fibre; 4 g Protein; 343 mg Sodium

Pictured on page 35.

Don't discard the drippings from your barbecued roast. Use them in this delicious recipe. Cook the Yorkshire pudding on the barbecue before slicing the roast.

Yorkshire Pudding

All-purpose flour	1 cup	250 mL
Milk	1 cup	250 mL
Large eggs	2	2
Salt	1/2 tsp.	2 mL
Cooking oil (or roast beef drippings)	2 tbsp.	30 mL

Beat first 4 ingredients in small bowl until smooth.

Spread cooking oil evenly in 9 x 9 inch (22 x 22 cm) shallow pan. Preheat barbecue to high. Place pan on 1 side of ungreased grill. Turn off burner under pan, turning opposite burner down to medium-high. Heat cooking oil until hot. Pour batter into pan. Spread evenly. Close lid. Cook for about 30 minutes, rotating pan at halftime, until lightly golden. Cuts into 9 pieces.

1 piece: 109 Calories; 4.6 g Total Fat (2.3 g Mono, 1.1 g Poly, 0.8 g Sat); 49 mg Cholesterol; 13 g Carbohydrate; trace Fibre; 4 g Protein; 160 mg Sodium

Pictured on page 35.

Top: Chili Herb Bread, this page
Bottom: Yorkshire Pudding, above

Fresh, grilled vegetables are tossed with a flavourful pesto in this appetizing salad your guests will love.

note

To toast nuts, spread evenly in ungreased shallow pan. Bake in 350°F (175°C) oven for 5 to 10 minutes, stirring or shaking often, until desired doneness.

Grilled Pesto Vegetable Salad

Green medium peppers, quartered, seeds and ribs removed	2	2
Red medium peppers, quartered, seeds and ribs removed	2	2
Medium zucchini (with peel), cut lengthwise into 1/4 inch (6 mm) thick slices	3	3
Red medium onions, each cut into 8 wedges	2	2
SPINACH PESTO		
Fresh spinach, stems removed, lightly packed	1 cup	250 mL
Pine nuts, toasted (see Note)	1/4 cup	60 mL
Grated Parmesan cheese	1/4 cup	60 mL
Olive (or cooking) oil	1/4 cup	60 mL
Balsamic vinegar	1 tbsp.	15 mL
Granulated sugar	1 tsp.	5 mL
Salt	1/4 tsp.	1 mL

Preheat barbecue to high. Arrange green and red peppers, skin-side down, on greased grill. Cook for 10 to 15 minutes until skins are blistered and blackened. Remove to medium bowl. Cover with plastic wrap. Let sweat for about 15 minutes until cool enough to handle. Peel and discard skins. Cut into 1/2 inch (12 mm) wide slices. Transfer to large bowl.

Cook zucchini and onion on greased grill for 3 to 5 minutes per side until tender-crisp and grill marks appear. Add to pepper. Toss gently.

Spinach Pesto: Process all 7 ingredients in blender or food processor until smooth. Makes about 2/3 cup (150 mL) pesto. Spoon over pepper mixture. Toss. Makes about 6 cups (1.5 L) salad. Serves 4.

1 serving: 304 Calories; 22.4 g Total Fat (13.3 g Mono, 3.8 g Poly, 4.2 g Sat); 5 mg Cholesterol; 23 g Carbohydrate; 7 g Fibre; 9 g Protein; 293 mg Sodium

Pictured on page 37.

A colourful, tangy salad that's perfect for company.

note

To toast nuts, spread evenly in ungreased shallow pan. Bake in 350°F (175°C) oven for 5 to 10 minutes, stirring or shaking often, until desired doneness.

Chicken And Artichoke Salad

BALSAMIC MARINADE

Olive (or cooking) oil	1/3 cup	75 mL
Balsamic vinegar	1/4 cup	60 mL
Liquid honey	2 tbsp.	30 mL
Chopped fresh basil (or 3/4 tsp., 4 mL, dried)	1 tbsp.	15 mL
Garlic cloves, minced (or 1/2 tsp., 2 mL, powder)	2	2
Lemon pepper	1 tsp.	5 mL
Boneless, skinless chicken breast halves	3/4 lb.	340 g
Large red onion, cut into 8 wedges	1	1
Bag of fresh spinach (about 3 1/2 cups, 875 mL, stems removed, lightly packed)	6 oz.	170 g
Can of artichoke hearts, drained and coarsely chopped	14 oz.	398 mL
Halved cherry tomatoes	1 cup	250 mL
Chopped walnuts, toasted (see Note)	1 cup	250 mL
Crumbled feta cheese (about 4 oz., 113 g)	3/4 cup	175 mL

Balsamic Marinade: Combine first 6 ingredients in jar with tight-fitting lid. Shake well. Makes about 3/4 cup (175 mL) marinade.

Place chicken in large resealable freezer bag. Pour 1/2 of marinade over top. Seal bag. Turn until coated. Marinate in refrigerator for 3 hours. Drain and discard marinade. Preheat barbecue to medium. Cook chicken on greased grill for about 5 minutes per side until no longer pink inside. Chop coarsely. Transfer to large bowl.

Cook onion on greased grill for about 10 minutes, turning once, until softened and grill marks appear. Add to chicken.

Add remaining 5 ingredients. Toss. Drizzle with remaining marinade. Toss. Makes about 11 cups (2.75 L) salad. Serves 6.

1 serving: 369 Calories; 24.4 g Total Fat (8.7 g Mono, 9.3 g Poly, 4.9 g Sat); 58 mg Cholesterol; 15 g Carbohydrate; 4 g Fibre; 26 g Protein; 459 mg Sodium

Pictured on page 39.

The dramatic colours of this salad are unique and visually striking. The lively citrus flavour will awaken your taste buds.

Fennel And Sausage Salad

ORANGE DRESSING

Olive (or cooking) oil	1/2 cup	125 mL
Red wine vinegar	1/4 cup	60 mL
Orange juice	1/4 cup	60 mL
Garlic clove, minced (or 1/4 tsp., 1 mL, powder)	1	1
Salt	1/4 tsp.	1 mL
Pepper, just a pinch		
Sultana raisins	1/2 cup	125 mL
Thick pork sausages (about 12 oz., 340 g)	4	4
Medium oranges, peeled and segmented	2 – 3	2 – 3
Head of radicchio, chopped or torn	1	1
Fennel bulb (white part only), thinly sliced	1	1
Pine nuts, toasted (see Note)	1/2 cup	125 mL

Orange Dressing: Combine first 6 ingredients in jar with tight-fitting lid. Shake well. Makes about 1 cup (250 mL) dressing.

Measure raisins into small bowl. Add 1/2 of dressing. Stir. Cover. Let stand for 30 minutes.

Preheat barbecue to medium. Cook sausages on greased grill for about 20 minutes, turning occasionally, until no longer pink inside. Cut diagonally into 1 inch (2.5 cm) pieces. Transfer to large bowl.

Add raisin mixture and remaining 4 ingredients. Toss. Drizzle with remaining dressing. Toss. Makes about 10 cups (2.5 L) salad. Serves 6.

1 serving: 538 Calories; 43.4 g Total Fat (24.6 g Mono, 6.8 g Poly, 9.7 g Sat); 51 mg Cholesterol; 24 g Carbohydrate; 3 g Fibre; 18 g Protein; 736 mg Sodium

Pictured on page 43.

Mango Beef Salad

Lemon pepper	1 tbsp.	15 mL
Olive (or cooking) oil	2 tsp.	10 mL
Garlic clove, minced (or 1/4 tsp., 1 mL, powder)	1	1
Boneless strip loin steaks (about 10 oz., 285 g, each)	2	2
Mixed salad greens, lightly packed	5 cups	1.25 L
Can of sliced mango with syrup, drained and coarsely chopped	14 oz.	398 mL
Cashews, toasted (see Note) and coarsely chopped	1/2 cup	125 mL
Bacon slices, cooked crisp and crumbled	8	8
MAPLE DRESSING		
Peanut (or cooking) oil	1/3 cup	75 mL
Red wine vinegar	2 tbsp.	30 mL
Maple (or maple-flavoured) syrup	2 tbsp.	30 mL
Soy sauce	2 tsp.	10 mL
Salt	1/4 tsp.	1 mL

Combine first 3 ingredients in small bowl.

Divide and spread evenly on both sides of each steak. Preheat barbecue to medium-high. Cook steaks on greased grill for about 5 minutes per side until desired doneness. Let stand for
10 minutes. Slice into 1/8 inch (3 mm) thick slices. Transfer to large bowl.

Add next 4 ingredients. Toss gently.

Maple Dressing: Combine all 5 ingredients in jar with tight-fitting lid. Shake well. Makes about 2/3 cup (150 mL) dressing. Pour over steak mixture. Toss gently. Makes about 11 cups (2.75 L) salad. Serves 8.

1 serving: 313 Calories; 22.7 g Total Fat (11.2 g Mono, 4.4 g Poly, 5.6 g Sat); 37 mg Cholesterol; 12 g Carbohydrate; 1 g Fibre; 16 g Protein; 740 mg Sodium

Pictured on page 43.

Smoky bacon is a nice addition to tangy mangoes, crisp vegetables and juicy steak. This will become a favourite!

note

To toast nuts, spread evenly in ungreased shallow pan. Bake in 350°F (175°C) oven for 5 to 10 minutes, stirring or shaking often, until desired doneness.

Photo Legend, next page

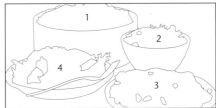

1. Veggie Pasta Salad, page 44
2. Mango Beef Salad, this page
3. Fennel And Sausage Salad, page 40
4. Barbecued Pork Salad, page 45

Grilled vegetables tossed with pasta in a creamy sun-dried tomato sauce. Delicious!

Veggie Pasta Salad

Roma (plum) tomatoes, cut into wedges	8	8
Chopped green onion	1/2 cup	125 mL
Olive (or cooking) oil	2 tbsp.	30 mL
Balsamic vinegar	2 tbsp.	30 mL
Garlic clove, minced (or 1/4 tsp., 1 mL, powder)	1	1
Italian no-salt seasoning (such as Mrs. Dash)	1/2 tsp.	2 mL
Granulated sugar	1/2 tsp.	2 mL
Salt, sprinkle		
Pepper, sprinkle		
Large red peppers, quartered, seeds and ribs removed	2	2
Medium zucchini (with peel), cut lengthwise into 1/4 inch (6 mm) thick slices	2	2
Eggplant (with peel), cut lengthwise into 1/4 inch (6 mm) thick slices	1	1
Cooked penne pasta (about 2 cups, 500 mL, uncooked), chilled	4 cups	1 L
Sour cream	1/3 cup	75 mL
Sun-dried tomato pesto	1/4 cup	60 mL

Put first 9 ingredients into medium bowl. Stir. Transfer to greased 8 x 8 inch (20 x 20 cm) foil pan. Preheat barbecue to medium-high. Place pan on ungreased grill. Close lid. Cook for about 15 minutes, stirring occasionally, until tomato is softened. Transfer tomato mixture with slotted spoon to large bowl. Discard liquid.

Cook red peppers on greased grill for about 15 minutes, turning occasionally, until grill marks appear and skins are slightly blackened. Chop coarsely. Add to tomato mixture.

Cook zucchini and eggplant slices on greased grill for 3 to 4 minutes per side until softened and grill marks appear. Chop coarsely. Add to tomato mixture. Add pasta. Toss gently.

Combine sour cream and pesto in small bowl. Add to pasta mixture. Toss gently. Makes about 10 cups (2.5 L) salad. Serves 6.

1 serving: 292 Calories; 8.1 g Total Fat (4.1 g Mono, 1.1 g Poly, 2 g Sat); 5 mg Cholesterol; 50 g Carbohydrate; 7 g Fibre; 9 g Protein; 79 mg Sodium

Pictured on pages 42/43.

Barbecued Pork Salad

Small oranges, peeled and white pith removed, thinly sliced	4	4
Thinly sliced red onion	2/3 cup	150 mL
ORANGE DRESSING		
Olive (or cooking) oil	1/3 cup	75 mL
Orange juice	1/4 cup	60 mL
Apple cider vinegar	3 tbsp.	50 mL
Liquid honey	1 tbsp.	15 mL
Grated orange zest	1/2 tsp.	2 mL
Dried basil	1/2 tsp.	2 mL
Garlic powder	1/8 tsp.	0.5 mL
Salt	1/4 tsp.	1 mL
Pepper, sprinkle		
Pork tenderloin, trimmed of fat	1 lb.	454 g
Garlic and herb no-salt seasoning (such as Mrs. Dash)	1 tsp.	5 mL
Pepper, sprinkle		
Mixed salad greens, lightly packed	10 cups	2.5 L

Spiced strips of pork and tangy orange dressing make salad greens delightful. Serve with crusty bread—yum!

Place orange slices and onion in large bowl. Toss gently.

Orange Dressing: Process first 9 ingredients in blender or food processor until smooth. Makes about 1 cup (250 mL) dressing. Pour over orange mixture. Toss gently. Cover. Chill for 2 hours.

Cut tenderloin almost in half lengthwise, but not quite through to other side. Press open to flatten. Sprinkle both sides with seasoning and pepper. Preheat barbecue to medium. Place tenderloin on greased grill. Close lid. Cook for 15 to 20 minutes, turning once, until meat thermometer inserted into thickest part of tenderloin reads 155°F (68°C). Remove from heat. Cover with foil. Let stand for 10 minutes. Internal temperature should rise to at least 160°F (70°C).

Add salad greens to orange mixture. Toss gently. Divide among 4 individual salad plates. Cut tenderloin into 1/4 inch (6 mm) thick slices. Arrange 4 to 5 slices of pork on top of each salad. Serves 4.

1 serving: 423 Calories; 24.3 g Total Fat (16.1 g Mono, 2.2 g Poly, 4.2 g Sat); 66 mg Cholesterol; 28 g Carbohydrate; 5 g Fibre; 26 g Protein; 222 mg Sodium

Pictured on page 42.

If you have travelled to Australia, you may have already experienced these hamburgers-with-the-works. Stacked high with sliced beets, bacon, egg, cheese, onions and more, this is a meal-in-a-bun!

Super Oz Burgers

Cooking oil	1 tbsp.	15 mL
Medium onions, thinly sliced	3	3
Large eggs (optional)	6	6
Finely chopped onion	3/4 cup	175 mL
Fresh bread crumbs	1/3 cup	75 mL
Large egg, fork-beaten	1	1
Barbecue sauce	2 tbsp.	30 mL
Salt	1/4 tsp.	1 mL
Pepper	1/4 tsp.	1 mL
Lean ground beef	1 lb.	454 g
Hamburger buns, split	6	6
Barbecue sauce	1/3 cup	75 mL
Can of sliced beets (12 – 18 slices)	14 oz.	398 mL
Cheddar cheese slices	6	6
Medium tomatoes, sliced	2	2
Bacon slices, cooked almost crisp	6	6
Green leaf lettuce leaves	6	6

Preheat barbecue to medium. Heat cooking oil on griddle or in large cast-iron pan on barbecue. Add onion. Cook for 5 to 10 minutes, stirring often, until softened. Remove onion to medium bowl. Cover to keep warm.

Reduce heat to medium-low. Break 3 eggs onto same griddle. When eggs start to set, add about 1 tbsp. (15 mL) water. Cover. Cook for about 1 minute until egg whites are set and yolks reach desired doneness, adding more water if needed. Remove eggs to plate. Cover to keep warm. Repeat with remaining 3 eggs.

Combine next 6 ingredients in large bowl. Add ground beef. Mix well. Divide and shape into 6 patties, about 5 inches (12.5 cm) in diameter. Increase heat to medium. Cook patties on greased grill for about 6 minutes per side until no longer pink inside.

Place buns, cut-side down, on greased grill. Toast until lightly browned.

Spread second amount of barbecue sauce on bottom half of each bun. Top each with patty, onion, beets, cheese, egg, tomato, bacon and lettuce. Cover with top half of each bun. Makes 6 burgers.

1 burger: 563 Calories; 30.6 g Total Fat (12.3 g Mono, 2.7 g Poly, 12.9 g Sat); 113 mg Cholesterol; 41 g Carbohydrate; 4 g Fibre; 31 g Protein; 1267 mg Sodium

Pictured on page 47.

The sweet taste of red peppers and honeyed pineapple sets this burger apart. Appealing in looks and taste.

Pineapple Pepper Burgers

Fresh bread crumbs	3/4 cup	175 mL
Finely chopped red pepper	3/4 cup	175 mL
Ketchup	1/3 cup	75 mL
Finely chopped onion	1/4 cup	60 mL
Sweet (or regular) chili sauce	2 tbsp.	30 mL
Chopped fresh cilantro or parsley (or 1 1/2 tsp., 7 mL, dried)	2 tbsp.	30 mL
Large egg	1	1
Salt	1 1/2 tsp.	7 mL
Pepper	1/4 tsp.	1 mL
Lean ground beef	1 1/2 lbs.	680 g
Pineapple slices	6	6
Soy sauce	2 tbsp.	30 mL
Liquid honey	1 tbsp.	15 mL
Kaiser buns, split	6	6
Red leaf lettuce leaves	6	6

Combine first 9 ingredients in large bowl.

Add ground beef. Mix well. Divide and shape into 6 patties, about 4 inches (10 cm) in diameter. Preheat barbecue to medium. Cook patties on greased grill for about 6 minutes per side until no longer pink inside.

Blot pineapple slices with paper towel. Combine soy sauce and honey in small bowl. Brush soy sauce mixture over both sides of each pineapple slice. Cook pineapple slices on greased grill for 2 to 3 minutes per side until grill marks appear.

Place buns, cut-side down, on greased grill. Toast until lightly browned. Place 1 lettuce leaf on bottom half of each bun. Top each with patty and pineapple slice. Cover with top half of each bun. Makes 6 burgers.

1 burger: 545 Calories; 21.3 g Total Fat (8.7 g Mono, 2.1 g Poly, 7.6 g Sat); 100 mg Cholesterol; 56 g Carbohydrate; 2 g Fibre; 31 g Protein; 1706 mg Sodium

Pictured on page 51.

Salmon Burgers

Peanut (or cooking) oil	1 tbsp.	15 mL
Medium onions, thinly sliced	2	2
Salt	1/8 tsp.	0.5 mL
Pepper	1/8 tsp.	0.5 mL
Salmon fillets, skin and bones removed, cut into 8 equal pieces (see Note)	2 lbs.	900 g
Peanut (or cooking) oil	1 tbsp.	15 mL
Lemon pepper	2 tbsp.	30 mL
Buns (your choice), split	8	8
Sour cream	1/2 cup	125 mL
Sweet (or regular) chili sauce	3 tbsp.	50 mL
Medium tomatoes, sliced	2	2

Thick, grilled salmon burgers that are a bit messy to eat—but so good!

note

For even cooking, choose fillets from the thicker centre of the salmon, rather than from the thinner tail end.

Preheat barbecue to medium-low. Heat first amount of peanut oil on griddle or in large cast-iron pan on barbecue. Add onion, salt and pepper. Cook for 5 to 10 minutes, stirring often, until onion is softened. Remove from heat. Keep warm.

Increase heat to medium. Brush salmon pieces with second amount of peanut oil. Sprinkle with lemon pepper. Cook salmon on greased grill for about 5 minutes per side, depending on thickness, until salmon flakes easily when tested with fork.

Place buns, cut-side down, on greased grill. Toast until lightly browned.

Combine sour cream and chili sauce in small bowl. Spread mixture on toasted sides of each bun.

Place 1 salmon piece on bottom half of each bun. Top each with onion mixture and tomato slices. Cover with top half of each bun. Makes 8 salmon burgers.

1 salmon burger: 410 Calories; 20.1 g Total Fat (7.7 g Mono, 6.1 g Poly, 4.9 g Sat); 72 mg Cholesterol; 29 g Carbohydrate; 1 g Fibre; 27 g Protein; 1333 mg Sodium

Pictured on page 50.

Photo Legend, next page

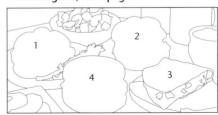

1. Salmon Burgers, this page
2. Pineapple Pepper Burgers, page 48
3. Grilled Quesadillas, page 52
4. Spicy Cheeseburgers, page 53

Crispy and golden on the outside with a spicy chicken filling on the inside.

Grilled Quesadillas

Sour cream	1/3 cup	75 mL
Chili sauce	2 tbsp.	30 mL
Chopped cooked chicken	3 cups	750 mL
Grated Monterey Jack cheese	1 2/3 cups	400 mL
Flour tortillas (10 inch, 25 cm, diameter)	4	4
Sliced pickled jalapeño peppers	1 – 2 tbsp.	15 – 30 mL
Medium tomatoes, seeds removed, diced	2	2
Finely chopped green onion	3 tbsp.	50 mL
Chopped fresh parsley (or 1 1/2 tsp., 7 mL, flakes)	2 tbsp.	30 mL
Cooking oil	1 tbsp.	15 mL

Combine sour cream and chili sauce in medium bowl. Add chicken. Toss until coated.

Divide and scatter cheese over 1/2 of each tortilla. Divide and spoon chicken mixture evenly over cheese.

Layer next 4 ingredients over chicken mixture. Fold each tortilla in half to enclose filling.

Preheat barbecue to medium. Brush tops of folded tortillas with 1/2 of cooking oil. Cook quesadillas, top-side down, on greased grill for 5 minutes. Brush with remaining cooking oil. Turn. Cook for about 5 minutes until crisp and golden and cheese is melted. Cut in half to serve. Serves 4.

1 serving: 656 Calories; 33.7 g Total Fat (11.8 g Mono, 5 g Poly, 14.4 g Sat); 152 mg Cholesterol; 36 g Carbohydrate; 3 g Fibre; 51 g Protein; 772 mg Sodium

Pictured on page 51.

Spicy Cheeseburgers

Fresh bread crumbs	1/4 cup	60 mL
Finely chopped red onion	1/4 cup	60 mL
Large egg, fork-beaten	1	1
Taco seasoning mix, stir before measuring	3 tbsp.	50 mL
Lime juice	2 tbsp.	30 mL
Chopped fresh oregano leaves (or 3/4 tsp., 4 mL, dried)	1 tbsp.	15 mL
Pepper, sprinkle		
Lean ground beef	1 lb.	454 g
Cheddar cheese slices	4	4
Hamburger buns, split	4	4
Sour cream	1/4 cup	60 mL
Medium tomato, thinly sliced	1	1
Salsa	1/4 cup	60 mL

Combine first 7 ingredients in medium bowl.

Add ground beef. Mix well. Divide and shape into 8 thin patties, about 5 inches (12.5 cm) in diameter.

Place 1 cheese slice on each of 4 patties. Top with remaining 4 patties. Pinch patty edges to enclose cheese. Preheat barbecue to medium-high. Cook patties on greased grill for about 6 minutes per side until no longer pink inside.

Place buns, cut-side down, on greased grill. Toast until lightly browned.

Place 1 patty on bottom half of each bun. Dollop each with 1 tbsp. (15 mL) sour cream. Top each with tomato slices and 1 tbsp. (15 mL) salsa. Cover with top half of each bun. Makes 4 cheeseburgers.

1 cheeseburger: 594 Calories; 33.4 g Total Fat (12.5 g Mono, 1.9 g Poly, 15.3 g Sat); 153 mg Cholesterol; 37 g Carbohydrate; 2 g Fibre; 36 g Protein; 1881 mg Sodium

Pictured on pages 50/51.

Taco seasoning and the tang of lime make these burgers Tex-Mex. The cheesy surprise inside will have everyone asking for seconds.

make ahead

Burger patties can be made ahead using fresh lean ground beef (not previously frozen). Place patties in airtight container, with waxed paper between each layer. Store in freezer for up to 2 months.

Tender, moist chicken with a hint of lime and just the right amount of spices to make it memorable.

variation

Brush wraps with 1 tbsp. (15 mL) cooking oil. Cook wraps on greased grill on medium for 5 to 7 minutes, turning occasionally, until crisp and golden.

Chicken Wraps

Chopped fresh cilantro or parsley (or 1 tbsp., 15 mL, dried)	1/4 cup	60 mL
Cooking oil	3 tbsp.	50 mL
Dried crushed chilies (optional)	2 tsp.	10 mL
Ground cumin	1 tsp.	5 mL
Garlic cloves, minced (or 1/2 tsp., 2 mL, powder)	2	2
Boneless, skinless chicken breast halves	1 lb.	454 g
Lime juice	1/4 cup	60 mL
Corn relish	1/4 cup	60 mL
Sour cream	1/4 cup	60 mL
Flour tortillas (10 inch, 25 cm, diameter)	4	4
Large ripe avocado, sliced	1	1
Red medium pepper, seeds and ribs removed, thinly sliced	1	1
Grated medium Cheddar cheese	1 cup	250 mL

Combine first 5 ingredients in medium bowl.

Add chicken. Stir. Cover with plastic wrap. Chill for at least 1 hour, stirring occasionally.

Add lime juice to chicken mixture. Stir. Drain and discard liquid. Preheat barbecue to medium. Cook chicken on greased grill for 10 to 15 minutes per side until no longer pink inside. Cut diagonally into thin slices. Cover to keep warm.

Measure corn relish and sour cream into small bowl. Stir. Spread about 2 tbsp. (30 mL) on each tortilla.

Divide and layer chicken, avocado, red pepper and cheese across centre of each tortilla, leaving 2 inches (5 cm) at each side. Fold sides over filling. Roll up from bottom to enclose filling. Slice in half diagonally. Serves 8.

1 serving: 337 Calories; 18.3 g Total Fat (8.2 g Mono, 3.3 g Poly, 5.4 g Sat); 59 mg Cholesterol; 21 g Carbohydrate; 2 g Fibre; 23 g Protein; 252 mg Sodium

Pictured on page 55.

Tasty grilled sandwiches to serve any time of the day! The sweet apple slices add crispness to the soft filling.

Apple And Cheese Grill

Hard margarine (or butter), softened	6 tbsp.	100 mL
Thick slices of raisin bread	8	8
Honey prepared mustard	1/4 cup	60 mL
Deli ham slices (about 6 oz., 170 g)	12	12
Large cooking apple (such as McIntosh), peeled and core removed, thinly sliced	1	1
Grated sharp Cheddar cheese	1 1/2 cups	375 mL

Spread margarine on 1 side of each bread slice. Place 4 bread slices, margarine-side down, on cutting board. Spread mustard on each.

Divide and layer ham slices, apple slices and cheese over each bread slice. Cover with remaining 4 bread slices, margarine-side up. Preheat barbecue to medium. Cook sandwiches on greased grill for about 6 minutes per side until golden and cheese is melted. Makes 4 sandwiches.

1 sandwich: 612 Calories; 39.4 g Total Fat (19.1 g Mono, 3.1 g Poly, 15.1 g Sat); 71 mg Cholesterol; 43 g Carbohydrate; 3 g Fibre; 23 g Protein; 1345 mg Sodium

Pictured on page 57.

Exotic flavours make this roast an impressive entrée. If the roast has excess fat, trim a piece off and use it to grease the grill.

serving suggestion

Serve with grilled red onion wedges.

Sesame Pepper-Crusted Beef Roast

Ingredient	Imperial	Metric
Rib-eye roast, trimmed of fat	3 lbs.	1.4 kg
Garlic cloves, halved	3	3
Olive (or cooking) oil	1 tbsp.	15 mL
Sesame seeds	1/4 cup	60 mL
Whole black peppercorns, cracked (see Note)	2 tbsp.	30 mL
Curry powder	2 tsp.	10 mL

Cut 6 shallow slits in roast at random. Insert garlic clove half into each slit. Brush olive oil over roast.

Combine remaining 3 ingredients in small bowl. Spread evenly on ungreased baking sheet. Roll roast in sesame seed mixture until coated. Preheat barbecue to medium-high. Place roast on 1 side of greased grill over drip pan. Turn off burner under roast, leaving opposite burner on medium-high. Close lid. Cook for 30 minutes. Reduce heat to medium. Cook for about 30 minutes until meat thermometer inserted into centre of roast reads 135°F (57°C) for rare to 165°F (74°C) for well done. Remove from heat. Cover with foil. Let stand for 10 minutes. Cut into 1/2 inch (12 mm) slices. Makes 12 servings (2 to 3 oz., 57 to 85 g each, cooked weight).

1 serving: 208 Calories; 10.4 g Total Fat (4.7 g Mono, 1.1 g Poly, 3.4 g Sat); 55 mg Cholesterol; 2 g Carbohydrate; 1 g Fibre; 25 g Protein; 72 mg Sodium

Pictured on page 59.

The most tender and juicy beef of all. Sure to please.

Grilled Beef Tenderloin

Hard margarine (or butter), melted	1/4 cup	60 mL
Red wine vinegar	1/2 tbsp.	7 mL
Worcestershire sauce	1 tsp.	5 mL
Beef bouillon powder	1/2 tsp.	2 mL
Beef tenderloin roast	2 1/4 lbs.	1 kg

Combine first 4 ingredients in small bowl.

Brush roast with margarine mixture. Preheat barbecue to high. Sear all sides of roast on greased grill. Reduce heat to medium-high. Move roast on 1 side of grill over drip pan. Turn off burner under roast, leaving opposite burner on medium-high. Close lid. Cook for about 60 minutes, turning occasionally and brushing with margarine mixture, until meat thermometer inserted into thickest part of roast reads 160°F (70°C) for medium, or until desired doneness. Cut into 1/2 inch (12 mm) slices. Makes 9 servings (2 to 3 oz., 57 to 85 g each, cooked weight).

1 serving: 178 Calories; 11 g Total Fat (5.6 g Mono, 0.8 g Poly, 3.2 g Sat); 44 mg Cholesterol; 0 g Carbohydrate; 0 g Fibre; 18 g Protein; 144 mg Sodium

Pictured on page 61.

A spicy steak that tastes great either warm or cold.

serving suggestion

Try it in a fajita or with roasted red peppers tossed with rice.

Spanish Sirloin

Paprika	2 tbsp.	30 mL
Lemon juice	2 tbsp.	30 mL
Garlic cloves, minced (or 1 tsp., 5 mL, powder)	4	4
Pepper	1 tsp.	5 mL
Beef sirloin tip steak	2 lbs.	900 g

Combine first 4 ingredients in small bowl.

Spread paprika mixture on both sides of steak. Preheat barbecue to medium. Cook steak on greased grill for 7 to 10 minutes per side until desired doneness. Remove from heat. Cover with foil. Let stand for 10 minutes. Cut into 1/4 inch (6 mm) thick slices. Makes 8 servings (2 to 3 oz., 57 to 85 g each, cooked weight).

1 serving: 154 Calories; 7.5 g Total Fat (3.2 g Mono, 0.4 g Poly, 2.9 g Sat); 49 mg Cholesterol; 2 g Carbohydrate; trace Fibre; 19 g Protein; 36 mg Sodium

Pictured on page 61.

Top: Grilled Beef Tenderloin, this page
Bottom: Spanish Sirloin, above

Crisp, fresh vegetables and deliciously barbecued steak—what a combination! Vegetables may need to be cooked in two batches.

Grilled Steak And Vegetables

BARBECUED VEGETABLES

Fresh whole white mushrooms	18 – 20	18 – 20
Medium zucchini (with peel), cut into 1/2 inch (12 mm) thick slices	2	2
Red medium onion, cut into wedges	1	1
Red medium pepper, cut into wedges, seeds and ribs removed	1	1
Yellow medium pepper, cut into wedges, seeds and ribs removed	1	1
Low-fat Italian dressing	3/4 cup	175 mL
Brown sugar, packed	2 tbsp.	30 mL
Olive (or cooking) oil	1 tbsp.	15 mL
Dry mustard	1 tsp.	5 mL
Ground coriander	1 tsp.	5 mL
Garlic cloves, minced (or 3/4 tsp., 4 mL, powder)	3	3
Salt	1 tsp.	5 mL
Pepper	2 tsp.	10 mL
Top sirloin, flank or inside round steak	2 lbs.	900 g

Barbecued Vegetables: Put first 5 ingredients into large bowl. Add dressing. Stir until coated. Cover with plastic wrap. Marinate in refrigerator for 2 to 3 hours, stirring occasionally. Drain and discard liquid from vegetables. Spread vegetable mixture evenly in large greased foil pan. Preheat barbecue to medium. Place pan on ungreased grill. Cook vegetables for 8 to 10 minutes, stirring occasionally, until tender-crisp. Remove from heat. Cover with foil to keep warm.

Combine next 7 ingredients in small bowl.

Spread brown sugar mixture over both sides of steak. Reduce heat to medium-low. Cook steak on greased grill for 7 to 10 minutes per side until desired doneness. Cut diagonally into 1/4 inch (6 mm) thick slices. Serve with vegetables. Makes 8 servings (2 to 3 oz., 57 to 85 g each, cooked weight).

1 serving: 217 Calories; 9.9 g Total Fat (4.7 g Mono, 0.7 g Poly, 3.2 g Sat); 50 mg Cholesterol; 12 g Carbohydrate; 2 g Fibre; 21 g Protein; 505 mg Sodium

Pictured on page 63.

Full-bodied marinade and tasty vegetables make these delicious. Marinate overnight for even more flavour if desired.

serving suggestion

Serve with rice or Potatoes On A Stick, page 108.

Barbecued Kabobs

SWEET SOY MARINADE

Soy sauce	1/3 cup	75 mL
Granulated sugar	2 tbsp.	30 mL
Cooking oil	2 tbsp.	30 mL
Worcestershire sauce	1 tbsp.	15 mL
Garlic clove, minced (or 1/4 tsp., 2 mL, powder)	1	1
Red wine vinegar	1 1/2 tbsp.	25 mL
Pepper	1/8 tsp.	0.5 mL
Beef top sirloin steak, cut into sixteen 1 inch (2.5 cm) cubes	1 1/4 lbs.	560 g
Fresh whole white mushrooms	8	8
Red medium onion, cut into 8 wedges	1	1
Green medium pepper, seeds and ribs removed, cut into 1 inch (2.5 cm) pieces	1	1
Red medium pepper, seeds and ribs removed, cut into 1 inch (2.5 cm) pieces	1	1
Cherry tomatoes	8	8
Small zucchini (with peel), halved lengthwise, each half cut into 8 pieces	1	1
Bamboo skewers (8 inch, 20 cm, length), soaked in water for 10 minutes	8	8

Sweet Soy Marinade: Combine first 7 ingredients in large bowl. Makes about 1/2 cup (125 mL) marinade.

Add beef. Stir until coated. Cover with plastic wrap. Marinate in refrigerator for 30 minutes, stirring occasionally. Drain, reserving marinade in small saucepan. Bring reserved marinade to a boil on medium. Reduce heat to medium-low. Simmer, uncovered, for at least 5 minutes.

Thread beef and vegetables alternately onto skewers. Preheat barbecue to medium-high. Cook kabobs on greased grill for about 20 minutes, turning occasionally and brushing with reserved marinade, until desired doneness. Makes 8 kabobs.

1 kabob: 167 Calories; 8.2 g Total Fat (4 g Mono, 1.3 g Poly, 2.1 g Sat); 31 mg Cholesterol; 10 g Carbohydrate; 1 g Fibre; 14 g Protein; 771 mg Sodium

Pictured on page 65.

When rib lovers crave meaty, sticky ribs, these are the kind they're thinking about. Add a chopped fresh chili pepper or two if you can stand the heat.

Teriyaki Ribs

Beef ribs, whole slab	5 1/2 lbs.	2.7 kg
Teriyaki sauce	1/2 cup	125 mL
Liquid honey	1/2 cup	125 mL
Dijon mustard (with whole seeds)	1/3 cup	75 mL
Worcestershire sauce	1/4 cup	60 mL
Hot pepper sauce	1 tbsp.	15 mL
Garlic cloves, minced (or 1 tsp., 5 mL, powder)	4	4

Place ribs in shallow baking dish.

Combine remaining 6 ingredients in small bowl. Makes about 1 1/2 cups (375 mL) marinade. Pour over ribs. Turn until coated. Cover with plastic wrap. Marinate in refrigerator for at least 6 hours or overnight, turning occasionally. Drain, reserving marinade in small saucepan. Bring reserved marinade to a boil on medium. Reduce heat to medium-low. Simmer, uncovered, for at least 5 minutes. Preheat barbecue to medium-low. Place ribs on 1 side of greased grill over drip pan. Turn off burner under ribs, leaving opposite burner on medium-low. Close lid. Cook for about 1 1/2 hours, turning occasionally and brushing with reserved marinade, until tender. Serves 8.

1 serving: 390 Calories; 16.8 g Total Fat (7.2 g Mono, 0.9 g Poly, 7 g Sat); 77 mg Cholesterol; 27 g Carbohydrate; trace Fibre; 33 g Protein; 1074 mg Sodium

Pictured on front cover.

Spicy, thick tomato marinade flavours this tender beef. Allow plenty of time to marinate.

Savoury Short Ribs

TOMATO MARINADE

Can of tomato sauce	7 1/2 oz.	213 mL
Apple cider vinegar	1/2 cup	125 mL
Cooking oil	1/4 cup	60 mL
Granulated sugar	1 1/2 tbsp.	25 mL
Dry onion flakes	1 tbsp.	15 mL
Worcestershire sauce	2 tsp.	10 mL
Prepared mustard	1 tsp.	5 mL
Chili powder	1 tsp.	5 mL
Pepper	1/2 tsp.	2 mL
Garlic powder	1/4 tsp.	1 mL

(continued on next page)

| Beef short ribs, bone-in | 3 lbs. | 1.4 kg |

Tomato Marinade: Combine first 10 ingredients in small bowl. Makes about 1 3/4 cups (425 mL) marinade.

Place short ribs in shallow baking dish. Pour marinade over ribs. Turn until coated. Cover with plastic wrap. Marinate in refrigerator for at least 6 hours or overnight, turning occasionally. Drain, reserving marinade in small saucepan. Bring reserved marinade to a boil on medium. Reduce heat to medium-low. Simmer, uncovered, for at least 5 minutes. Let ribs stand until room temperature before cooking. Preheat barbecue to low. Place ribs on greased grill. Close lid. Cook for about 45 minutes, turning occasionally and brushing with reserved marinade, until tender. Serves 4.

1 serving: 480 Calories; 32.4 g Total Fat (16.3 g Mono, 4.9 g Poly, 8.6 g Sat); 84 mg Cholesterol; 13 g Carbohydrate; 1 g Fibre; 35 g Protein; 455 mg Sodium

Pictured below.

Mustard Seasoned Steak

Visible mustard seeds make this steak pleasing to look at, as well as delicious.

MUSTARD WINE MARINADE

Dijon mustard (with whole seeds)	1/4 cup	60 mL
Dry white (or alcohol-free) wine	1/4 cup	60 mL
Apple cider vinegar	2 tbsp.	30 mL
Cooking oil	2 tbsp.	30 mL
Finely chopped fresh rosemary (or 3/4 tsp., 4 mL, dried, crushed)	1 tbsp.	15 mL
Pepper, sprinkle		
Flank steak	1 1/2 lbs.	680 g

Mustard Wine Marinade: Combine first 6 ingredients in small bowl. Makes about 2/3 cup (150 mL) marinade.

Put steak into large resealable freezer bag. Pour marinade over top. Seal bag. Turn until coated. Marinate in refrigerator for at least 6 hours or overnight, turning occasionally. Drain, reserving marinade in small saucepan. Bring reserved marinade to a boil on medium. Reduce heat to medium-low. Simmer, uncovered, for at least 5 minutes. Preheat barbecue to high. Cook steak on greased grill for 5 to 7 minutes per side, turning occasionally and brushing with reserved marinade, until desired doneness. Remove from heat. Cover with foil. Let stand for 10 minutes. Cut diagonally into very thin slices. Makes 6 servings (2 to 3 oz., 57 to 85 g each, cooked weight).

1 serving: 249 Calories; 14.1 g Total Fat (6.4 g Mono, 2.1 g Poly, 4.2 g Sat); 46 mg Cholesterol; 1 g Carbohydrate; 0 g Fibre; 27 g Protein; 198 mg Sodium

Pictured on page 69.

Barbecued Meatloaf

This tender and moist loaf tastes great hot off the barbecue.

Lean ground beef	1 1/2 lbs.	680 g
Finely chopped onion	1/3 cup	75 mL
Salt	1 1/2 tsp.	7 mL
Pepper	1/4 tsp.	1 mL
Chili sauce	1 cup	250 mL
Brown sugar, packed	1/4 cup	60 mL
White vinegar	2 tbsp.	30 mL
Dry mustard	1 tsp.	5 mL
Drops of hot pepper sauce	3	3

(continued on next page)

Put first 4 ingredients into medium bowl. Mix well. Shape into flattened rectangular loaf. Place on ungreased sheet of heavy-duty (or double layer of regular) foil. Fold edges of foil to enclose. Preheat barbecue to medium. Place meatloaf in foil on 1 side of ungreased grill. Turn off burner under meatloaf, leaving opposite burner on medium. Close lid. Cook for about 1 1/4 hours until meatloaf is no longer pink inside.

Combine remaining 5 ingredients in separate medium bowl. Remove meatloaf from grill. Open foil. Spread chili sauce mixture over meatloaf. Return to grill, leaving foil open. Close lid. Cook for about 15 minutes until sauce is bubbling. Serves 6.

1 serving: 338 Calories; 17.4 g Total Fat (7.6 g Mono, 0.8 g Poly, 6.9 g Sat); 64 mg Cholesterol; 23 g Carbohydrate; 3 g Fibre; 23 g Protein; 1317 mg Sodium

Pictured below.

Top: Barbecued Meatloaf, page 68
Bottom: Mustard Seasoned Steak, page 68

The tropical taste comes alive on the barbecue!

serving suggestion

Delicious served with Mushroom Packets, page 110, or Roasted Vegetable Mix, page 112. For garnish, add a few grilled lemon wedges.

Mango-Stuffed Chicken

Diced ripe mango (or 14 oz., 398 mL, can of sliced mango with syrup, drained and diced)	1 cup	250 mL
Finely chopped salted macadamia nuts (or almonds)	1/2 cup	125 mL
Thinly sliced green onion	2 tbsp.	30 mL
Grated lime (or lemon) zest	1/2 tsp.	2 mL
Curry powder	1/2 tsp.	2 mL
Whole roasting chicken	4 lbs.	1.8 kg
LIME YOGURT MARINADE		
Plain yogurt	1 1/2 cups	375 mL
Lime (or lemon) juice	1/4 cup	60 mL
Ground coriander	1 tbsp.	15 mL
Curry powder	1 tbsp.	15 mL
Finely grated, peeled gingerroot (or 1/2 tsp., 2 mL, ground ginger)	2 tsp.	10 mL
Garlic cloves, minced (or 1 tsp., 5 mL, powder)	4	4
Salt	1 tsp.	5 mL

Put first 5 ingredients into medium bowl. Stir.

Place chicken, backbone-up, on cutting board. Cut down both sides of backbone with kitchen shears or sharp knife to remove. Turn chicken over. Press chicken out flat. Carefully loosen skin but do not remove. Stuff mango mixture between meat and skin, spreading mixture as evenly as possible. Place stuffed chicken in large shallow baking dish.

Lime Yogurt Marinade: Combine all 7 ingredients in small bowl. Makes about 1 3/4 cups (425 mL) marinade. Pour over chicken. Turn until coated. Cover with plastic wrap. Marinate in refrigerator for at least 3 hours, turning occasionally. Drain and discard marinade. Preheat barbecue to medium. Place chicken, skin-side down, on 1 side of greased grill over drip pan. Turn off burner under chicken, leaving opposite burner on medium. Close lid. Cook for 45 minutes. Turn chicken over. Close lid. Cook for 45 to 50 minutes until meat thermometer inserted into breast (not stuffing) reads 180°F (82°C). Remove from heat. Cover with foil. Let stand for 15 minutes. Cut into serving-size portions. Serves 6.

1 serving: 399 Calories; 24.1 g Total Fat (12.2 g Mono, 3.7 g Poly, 5.9 g Sat); 107 mg Cholesterol; 10 g Carbohydrate; 2 g Fibre; 35 g Protein; 320 mg Sodium

Pictured on page 71.

The sauce takes on a pretty pink colour from the grenadine. Don't forget to eat the lettuce—it's delightfully refreshing with lemon sauce on it!

serving suggestion

Serve with rice and Barbecued Asparagus, page 110.

Lemon Chicken And Sauce

LEMON MARINADE

Frozen concentrated lemonade, thawed	1/4 cup	60 mL
Cooking oil	1 tbsp.	15 mL
Grenadine syrup	1 tbsp.	15 mL
Onion powder	1/2 tsp.	2 mL
Garlic salt	1/2 tsp.	2 mL
Boneless, skinless chicken breast halves (4 – 6 oz., 113 – 170 g, each)	4	4
Water	1/2 cup	125 mL
Frozen concentrated lemonade, thawed	1/4 cup	60 mL
Grenadine syrup	2 tbsp.	30 mL
Cornstarch	1 tbsp.	15 mL
Grated lemon zest	1 tsp.	5 mL
Chopped iceberg lettuce, lightly packed	2 cups	500 mL
Lemon slices, halved, for garnish		

Lemon Marinade: Combine first 5 ingredients in small bowl. Makes about 1/3 cup (75 mL) marinade.

Place chicken in large resealable freezer bag. Add marinade. Seal bag. Turn until coated. Marinate in refrigerator for at least 6 hours or overnight, turning occasionally. Drain and discard marinade. Preheat barbecue to medium. Place chicken on greased grill. Close lid. Cook for 20 to 25 minutes, turning occasionally, until no longer pink inside.

Combine next 5 ingredients in small saucepan. Heat and stir on medium for about 6 minutes until boiling and thickened. Makes about 2/3 cup (150 mL) sauce.

Arrange lettuce on 4 individual plates. Place 1 chicken breast half on top of lettuce on each plate. Spoon sauce over each chicken breast half.

Garnish each serving with lemon slices. Serves 4.

1 serving: 276 Calories; 4.2 g Total Fat (1.6 g Mono, 1.1 g Poly, 0.8 g Sat); 81 mg Cholesterol; 27 g Carbohydrate; trace Fibre; 32 g Protein; 90 mg Sodium

Pictured on page 73.

Skewers with turkey, pineapple and green pepper. Sweet and delicious.

serving suggestion

Serve with rice and fresh green salad on the side.

Teriyaki Turkey Skewers

HONEY TERIYAKI SAUCE

Teriyaki sauce	1/2 cup	125 mL
Liquid honey	2 tbsp.	30 mL
Ketchup	2 tbsp.	30 mL
Pepper	1 tsp.	5 mL
Garlic powder	1/2 tsp.	2 mL
Ground ginger	1/4 – 1/2 tsp.	1 – 2 mL
Cayenne pepper	1/8 – 1/4 tsp.	0.5 – 1 mL
Boneless, skinless turkey breast half, cut into 1 inch (2.5 cm) cubes	1 1/2 lbs.	680 g
Fresh pineapple, cut into 3/4 inch (2 cm) pieces	2 1/2 cups	625 mL
Green medium pepper, seeds and ribs removed, cut into 3/4 inch (2 cm) pieces	2 1/2 cups	625 mL
Bamboo skewers (12 inch, 30 cm, length), soaked in water for 10 minutes	12	12

Honey Teriyaki Sauce: Combine first 7 ingredients in small bowl. Makes about 3/4 cup (175 mL) sauce.

Thread turkey, pineapple and green pepper alternately onto skewers. Preheat barbecue to medium. Cook skewers on greased grill for 12 to 15 minutes, turning occasionally and brushing with sauce, until turkey is no longer pink inside. Makes 12 skewers.

1 skewer: 114 Calories; 0.5 g Total Fat (0.1 g Mono, 0.2 g Poly, 0.1 g Sat); 35 mg Cholesterol; 12 g Carbohydrate; 1 g Fibre; 15 g Protein; 545 mg Sodium

Pictured on page 75.

The olive oil and fresh herb filling in this roll keeps the turkey moist and succulent.

serving suggestion

Try this with Foiled Yams, page 109, or Roasted Vegetable Mix, page 112.

Herbed Turkey Roll

Boneless, skinless turkey breast half (about 1 1/2 lbs., 680 g)	1	1
Olive (or cooking) oil	3 tbsp.	50 mL
Garlic cloves, minced (or 1 tsp., 5 mL, powder)	4	4
Dijon mustard	1 tbsp.	15 mL
Chopped fresh parsley (or 3/4 tsp., 4 mL, flakes)	1 tbsp.	15 mL
Chopped fresh chives (or 3/4 tsp., 4 mL, dried)	1 tbsp.	15 mL
Fresh rosemary leaves (or 1/4 – 3/4 tsp., 2 – 4 mL, dried, crushed)	1 – 3 tsp.	5 – 15 mL
Salt	1 tsp.	5 mL
Pepper	1 tsp.	5 mL
Uncooked bacon slices	3 – 4	3 – 4

Butterfly turkey breast half by cutting horizontally through middle, not quite to other side. Spread open and pound with smooth side of mallet until thin, even thickness.

Combine next 8 ingredients in small bowl. Spread evenly on turkey breast half. Roll up tightly, starting from long edge. Secure with butcher's string.

Lay bacon slices over top of turkey roll. Preheat barbecue to medium. Place turkey roll on 1 side of greased grill over drip pan. Turn off burner under drip pan, leaving opposite burner on medium. Close lid. Cook for about 1 1/2 hours until turkey is no longer pink inside. Remove to platter. Remove and discard string. Discard bacon if desired. Slice turkey roll into 3/4 inch (2 cm) thick slices. Serves 4.

1 serving: 317 Calories; 14 g Total Fat (8.9 g Mono, 1.6 g Poly, 2.6 g Sat); 109 mg Cholesterol; 2 g Carbohydrate; trace Fibre; 44 g Protein; 806 mg Sodium

Pictured on page 77.

These tender, browned Cornish hens taste of apple and sage with a hint of cinnamon. A great meal for entertaining.

Roasted Cornish Hens

Cornish hens (about 1 1/2 lbs., 680 g, each)	2	2

BEER MARINADE

Beer (or alcohol-free beer)	1 cup	250 mL
Applesauce	1/2 cup	125 mL
Olive (or cooking) oil	2 tbsp.	30 mL
Liquid honey	2 tbsp.	30 mL
Paprika	1 tsp.	5 mL
Ground sage	3/4 tsp.	4 mL
Ground cinnamon	1/2 tsp.	2 mL
Salt	1/4 tsp.	1 mL

Place 1 Cornish hen, backbone-up, on cutting board. Cut down both sides of backbone with kitchen shears or sharp knife to remove. Turn hen over. Cut lengthwise through breast into halves. Repeat with remaining hen.

Beer Marinade: Combine all 8 ingredients in large bowl. Makes about 1 3/4 cups (425 mL) marinade. Add Cornish hen halves. Turn until coated. Cover with plastic wrap. Marinate in refrigerator for at least 6 hours or overnight, turning occasionally. Drain, reserving marinade in small saucepan. Bring reserved marinade to a boil on medium. Reduce heat to medium-low. Simmer, uncovered, for at least 5 minutes. Preheat barbecue to high. Place Cornish hen halves, bone-side down, on 1 side of greased grill. Turn off burner under hen halves, leaving opposite burner on medium. Brush hen halves with reserved marinade. Close lid. Cook for 20 minutes. Turn. Close lid. Cook for about 20 minutes, turning occasionally and brushing with marinade, until browned and no longer pink inside. Serves 4.

1 serving: 435 Calories; 27.8 g Total Fat (14.2 g Mono, 4.8 g Poly, 6.7 g Sat); 150 mg Cholesterol; 15 g Carbohydrate; 1 g Fibre; 26 g Protein; 226 mg Sodium

Pictured on page 79.

You will love the light smoky flavour of this salmon, perfectly complemented by delicately sweet maple syrup.

Cedar Plank Salmon

Cedar planks (see Note)	2	2
Water		
WHISKY MARINADE		
Canadian whisky (rye)	1 cup	250 mL
Maple (or maple-flavoured) syrup	1/2 cup	125 mL
Soy sauce	1/3 cup	75 mL
Olive (or cooking) oil	1/4 cup	60 mL
Parsley flakes	1/4 cup	60 mL
Sweet (or regular) chili sauce	3 tbsp.	50 mL
Pepper	1 tsp.	5 mL
Salmon fillets (about 4 oz., 113 g, each), or side of salmon (about 2 lbs., 900 g), skin removed, cut into 8 equal pieces	8	8

Place cedar planks in large container. Add enough water to cover. Weight planks with heavy cans to keep submerged. Let stand for at least 6 hours or overnight to soak.

Whisky Marinade: Combine first 7 ingredients in medium bowl. Makes about 2 1/4 cups (550 mL) marinade.

Place salmon in large shallow baking dish. Pour marinade over top. Turn until coated. Cover. Marinate in refrigerator for at least 30 minutes, turning occasionally. Drain and discard marinade. Preheat barbecue to medium-low. Place salmon on cedar planks on ungreased grill. Close lid. Cook for 15 to 30 minutes until salmon flakes easily when tested with fork. Serves 8.

1 serving: 260 Calories; 10.6 g Total Fat (4.9 g Mono, 3.2 g Poly, 1.6 g Sat); 62 mg Cholesterol; 9 g Carbohydrate; trace Fibre; 23 g Protein; 457 mg Sodium

Pictured on page 81.

This is a wonderful way to prepare a piece of whole salmon. Smothered in a buttery lemon barbecue sauce.

serving suggestion

Serve with wild rice and carrots for a "supreme" supper.

Salmon Supreme

LEMON BARBECUE SAUCE

Lemon juice	2/3 cup	150 mL
Hickory barbecue sauce	1/2 cup	125 mL
Butter (or hard margarine)	1/2 cup	125 mL
Finely chopped onion	1/4 cup	60 mL
Brown sugar, packed	1/2 tbsp.	7 mL
Garlic powder, just a pinch		
Centre section of whole salmon (with skin), cut lengthwise to backbone and opened flat	3 lbs.	1.4 kg

Lemon Barbecue Sauce: Combine first 6 ingredients in small saucepan. Bring to a boil on medium. Reduce heat to medium-low. Simmer, uncovered, for 20 to 30 minutes, stirring often, until onion is softened. Makes about 1 cup (250 mL) sauce.

Brush salmon flesh with 1/2 of sauce. Preheat barbecue to medium. Place salmon, flesh-side down, on greased grill. Close lid. Cook for 15 minutes. Turn. Brush salmon flesh with remaining 1/2 of sauce. Close lid. Cook for about 12 minutes, without turning, until salmon flakes easily when tested with fork. Cut into 10 equal portions. Serves 10.

1 serving: 275 Calories; 17.6 g Total Fat (5.4 g Mono, 3.5 g Poly, 7.3 g Sat); 92 mg Cholesterol; 4 g Carbohydrate; 1 g Fibre; 24 g Protein; 260 mg Sodium

Pictured on page 83.

Try salmon this way for a change. A treat to remember!

Teriyaki Salmon

TERIYAKI MARINADE

Soy sauce	3/4 cup	175 mL
Brown sugar, packed	1/2 cup	125 mL
Cooking oil	2 tbsp.	30 mL
Ground ginger	1/2 tsp.	2 mL
Garlic powder	1/4 tsp.	1 mL
Salmon steaks (or fillets), about 5 oz. (140 g) each	4	4

Teriyaki Marinade: Combine first 5 ingredients in small bowl. Makes about 1 cup (250 mL) marinade.

Place salmon steaks in large shallow baking dish. Pour marinade over top. Turn until coated. Cover. Marinate in refrigerator for 30 minutes, turning occasionally. Drain and discard marinade. Preheat barbecue to medium. Cook salmon steaks on greased grill for about 5 minutes per side until salmon flakes easily when tested with fork. Serves 4.

1 serving: 303 Calories; 12.3 g Total Fat (5 g Mono, 4.6 g Poly, 1.6 g Sat); 77 mg Cholesterol; 17 g Carbohydrate; trace Fibre; 30 g Protein; 1703 mg Sodium

Pictured on page 85.

Zesty lemon marinade perfectly accents this moist fish. Delicate sea bass should be turned carefully to avoid breaking.

Lemon Dill Bass

LEMON DILL MARINADE

Lemon juice	1/4 cup	60 mL
Olive (or cooking) oil	2 tbsp.	30 mL
Chopped fresh dill (or 1 1/4 tsp., 6 mL, dill weed)	1 1/2 tbsp.	25 mL
Chopped fresh chives (or 3/4 tsp., 4 mL, dried)	1 tbsp.	15 mL
Grated lemon zest	2 tsp.	10 mL
Paprika	1 tsp.	5 mL
Salt	1/2 tsp.	2 mL
Fresh (or frozen, thawed) sea bass steaks	1 1/4 lbs.	560 g

(continued on next page)

Lemon Dill Marinade: Combine first 7 ingredients in small bowl. Makes about 1/3 cup (75 mL) marinade.

Place bass steaks in shallow medium baking dish. Pour marinade over top. Turn until coated. Cover. Marinate in refrigerator for 30 minutes, turning occasionally. Drain and discard marinade. Preheat barbecue to medium. Cook bass steaks on greased grill for 15 to 20 minutes, turning once, until bass flakes easily when tested with fork. Cut bass steaks into 4 equal portions, removing and discarding skin and bones. Serves 4.

1 serving: 170 Calories; 6.3 g Total Fat (3.1 g Mono, 1.4 g Poly, 1.2 g Sat); 57 mg Cholesterol; 1 g Carbohydrate; trace Fibre; 26 g Protein; 244 mg Sodium

Pictured below.

Left: Teriyaki Salmon, page 84
Right: Lemon Dill Bass, page 84

Slightly sweet apricot and dill filling is a delectable complement to trout.

note

To toast nuts, spread evenly in ungreased shallow pan. Bake in 350°F (175°C) oven for 5 to 10 minutes, stirring or shaking often, until desired doneness.

Apricot-Stuffed Trout

Cooking oil	2 tsp.	10 mL
Finely chopped red onion	1/4 cup	60 mL
Cooked jasmine (or long grain white) rice	1/2 cup	125 mL
Finely chopped pecans, toasted (see Note)	2 tbsp.	30 mL
Orange juice	1 tbsp.	15 mL
Finely chopped dried apricot	1 tbsp.	15 mL
Chopped fresh dill (or 1/2 tsp., 2 mL, dill weed)	1 1/2 tsp.	7 mL
Salt	1/4 tsp.	1 mL
Pepper, just a pinch		
Whole trout (about 10 oz., 280 g, each), pan ready	2	2

Heat cooking oil in small frying pan on medium. Add onion. Cook for 5 to 10 minutes, stirring often, until softened. Transfer to large bowl.

Add next 7 ingredients. Stir well.

Rinse inside of each trout. Pat dry with paper towels. Divide and spoon rice mixture into each trout. Spread evenly. Tie each with butcher's string or secure with metal skewers to enclose filling. Preheat barbecue to medium-low. Place trout on greased grill. Close lid. Cook for 5 to 6 minutes per side until trout flakes easily when tested with fork. Serves 4.

1 serving: 236 Calories; 11.4 g Total Fat (6.1 g Mono, 2.8 g Poly, 1.5 g Sat); 57 mg Cholesterol; 11 g Carbohydrate; trace Fibre; 22 g Protein; 200 mg Sodium

Pictured on page 87.

These tender, grilled scallops, delicately coated with lightly spiced honey mustard sauce, are sure to impress!

Sweet Scallop Skewers

Fresh (or frozen, thawed) large sea scallops, cut into 1/2 inch (12 mm) thick pieces	1 lb.	454 g
Bamboo skewers (8 inch, 20 cm, length), soaked in water for 10 minutes	8	8
Liquid honey	2 tbsp.	30 mL
Dijon mustard	2 tbsp.	30 mL
Grated orange zest	1/4 tsp.	1 mL
Chili powder	1/4 tsp.	1 mL
Salt	1/4 tsp.	1 mL

Thread scallop pieces onto skewers.

Combine remaining 5 ingredients in small bowl. Brush scallop pieces with honey mixture. Preheat barbecue to medium. Cook skewers on greased grill for about 8 minutes, turning occasionally and brushing with remaining honey mixture, until scallop pieces are opaque. Do not overcook. Makes 8 skewers.

1 skewer: 70 Calories; 0.7 g Total Fat (0.1 g Mono, 0.3 g Poly, 0.1 g Sat); 19 mg Cholesterol; 6 g Carbohydrate; trace Fibre; 10 g Protein; 219 mg Sodium

Pictured on page 89.

Colourful cantaloupe salsa is a delightful condiment for tuna. Avoid overcooking tuna to prevent drying.

Tuna Skewers

CANTALOUPE SALSA

Diced cantaloupe	1 cup	250 mL
Finely chopped green onion	2 tbsp.	30 mL
Lemon juice	1 1/2 tbsp.	25 mL
Cooking oil	1 tbsp.	15 mL
Chopped fresh basil	1 tbsp.	15 mL
Salt	1/4 tsp.	1 mL
Pepper, just a pinch		
Lemon juice	1/4 cup	60 mL
Soy sauce	2 tbsp.	30 mL
Brown sugar, packed	2 tbsp.	30 mL
Garlic clove, minced (or 1/4 tsp., 1 mL, powder)	1	1

(continued on next page)

| Tuna steaks (or fillets), cut into 1 inch (2.5 cm) cubes | 1 3/4 lbs. | 790 g |
| Bamboo skewers (8 inch, 20 cm, length), soaked in water for 10 minutes | 8 | 8 |

Cantaloupe Salsa: Combine first 7 ingredients in medium bowl. Cover. Chill for 2 hours to blend flavours. Drain and discard liquid. Transfer solids to small serving dish. Makes about 1 cup (250 mL) salsa.

Combine next 4 ingredients in small bowl.

Thread tuna cubes onto skewers. Brush with lemon juice mixture. Preheat barbecue to medium. Cook skewers on greased grill for about 5 minutes, turning occasionally and brushing with remaining lemon juice mixture, until tuna is firm and no longer opaque. Serve with Cantaloupe Salsa. Serves 8.

1 serving: 141 Calories; 1.9 g Total Fat (0.7 g Mono, 0.5 g Poly, 0.3 g Sat); 44 mg Cholesterol; 7 g Carbohydrate; trace Fibre; 24 g Protein; 340 mg Sodium

Pictured below.

Left: Tuna Skewers, page 88
Top Centre: Cantaloupe Salsa, psge 88
Right: Sweet Scallop Skewers, page 88

Sweet, tangy marinade makes pork tenderloin especially tasty!

Barbecued Tenderloin Slices

CHILI MARINADE

Sweet (or regular) chili sauce	1/2 cup	125 mL
Ketchup	1/2 cup	125 mL
Apple cider vinegar	1/2 cup	125 mL
Fancy (mild) molasses	1/3 cup	75 mL
Lemon juice	1 tbsp.	15 mL
Worcestershire sauce	2 tsp.	10 mL
Dry mustard	2 tsp.	10 mL
Pork tenderloins (about 1 lb., 454 g, each), trimmed of fat	2	2

Chili Marinade: Combine first 7 ingredients in small bowl. Makes about 2 cups (500 mL) marinade.

Cut each tenderloin almost in half lengthwise, but not quite through to other side. Press open to flatten. Place in large resealable freezer bag. Pour 1/2 of marinade over tenderloins. Chill remaining marinade. Seal bag. Turn until coated. Marinate in refrigerator for at least 4 hours, turning occasionally. Drain and discard marinade. Preheat barbecue to medium. Place tenderloins on greased grill. Close lid. Cook for about 20 minutes, turning occasionally (see Note) and brushing with remaining marinade, until meat thermometer inserted into thickest part of tenderloin reads 155°F (68°C). Remove from heat. Cover with foil. Let stand for 10 minutes. Internal temperature should rise to at least 160°F (70°C). Cut each tenderloin into 1/2 inch (12 mm) thick slices. Serves 8.

1 serving: 199 Calories; 5 g Total Fat (2.2 g Mono, 0.4 g Poly, 1.6 g Sat); 66 mg Cholesterol; 15 g Carbohydrate; 1 g Fibre; 23 g Protein; 378 mg Sodium

Pictured on page 91.

The peppery marinade is a real winner! Marinate pork overnight to infuse with even more flavour.

serving suggestion

Serve with Veggie Pasta Salad, page 44, or Mushroom Packets, page 110.

Best Pork Chops

GARLIC MARINADE

Water	1/2 cup	125 mL
Soy sauce	1/3 cup	75 mL
Cooking oil	1/4 cup	60 mL
Lemon pepper	3 tbsp.	50 mL
Garlic cloves, minced (or 1/2 tsp., 2 mL, powder)	2	2
Bone-in pork chops (about 2 1/2 lbs., 1.1 kg), trimmed of fat	6	6

Garlic Marinade: Combine first 5 ingredients in small bowl. Makes about 1 cup (250 mL) marinade.

Place pork chops in single layer in large shallow baking dish. Pour marinade over top. Turn until coated. Cover. Marinate in refrigerator for 45 minutes, turning occasionally. Drain, reserving marinade in small saucepan. Bring reserved marinade to a boil on medium. Reduce heat to medium-low. Simmer, uncovered, for at least 5 minutes. Preheat barbecue to medium. Cook pork chops on greased grill for about 25 minutes, turning once and brushing with reserved marinade, until desired doneness. Serves 6.

1 serving: 274 Calories; 15.9 g Total Fat (8.5 g Mono, 3.5 g Poly, 2.8 g Sat); 77 mg Cholesterol; 3 g Carbohydrate; trace Fibre; 29 g Protein; 2824 mg Sodium

Pictured on page 95.

Minted Lamb Chops

Red wine and a hint of mint make a delectable marinade for tender lamb. Use your favourite cut of lamb chops and adjust cooking time to suit.

RED WINE MARINADE

Dry red (or alcohol-free) wine	1/2 cup	125 mL
Mint jelly	1/3 cup	75 mL
Lemon juice	3 tbsp.	50 mL
Finely grated, peeled gingerroot (or 1/8 tsp., 0.5 mL, ground ginger)	1/2 tsp.	2 mL
Salt	1/2 tsp.	2 mL
Pepper	1/2 tsp.	2 mL
Lamb loin chops (2 – 2 1/2 lbs., 900 g – 1.1 kg)	12	12

Red Wine Marinade: Heat and stir first 6 ingredients in medium saucepan on medium for about 5 minutes until smooth. Cool. Makes about 1 cup (250 mL) marinade.

Arrange lamb chops in single layer in large shallow baking dish. Pour marinade over top. Turn until coated. Cover. Marinate in refrigerator for 6 hours or overnight, turning occasionally. Drain and discard marinade. Preheat barbecue to medium. Cook lamb chops on greased grill for 5 to 7 minutes per side until desired doneness. Serves 6.

1 serving: 436 Calories; 29.6 g Total Fat (12.4 g Mono, 2.2 g Poly, 12.6 g Sat); 128 mg Cholesterol; 7 g Carbohydrate; trace Fibre; 32 g Protein; 202 mg Sodium

Pictured on pages 94/95.

Photo Legend, next page

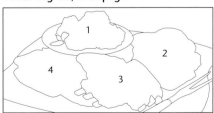

1. Minted Lamb Chops, this page
2. Best Pork Chops, page 92
3. Java Ribs, page 97
4. Honey Ham Steaks, page 96

A foolproof meal that is quick and easy to prepare.

serving suggestion

Serve with Quick Corn, page 102, or Veggie Bread Kabobs, page 104.

Honey Ham Steaks

HONEY MUSTARD SAUCE

Brown sugar, packed	1/4 cup	60 mL
Hard margarine (or butter)	1/4 cup	60 mL
Liquid honey	1 tbsp.	15 mL
Soy sauce	1 tsp.	5 mL
Prepared mustard	1 tsp.	5 mL
Ham steaks, trimmed of fat (about 2 lbs., 900 g)	8	8

Honey Mustard Sauce: Heat and stir first 5 ingredients in small saucepan on medium for about 5 minutes until sugar is dissolved. Makes about 3/4 cup (175 mL) sauce. Transfer 1/2 cup (125 mL) sauce to small serving dish. Set aside to serve with ham.

Preheat barbecue to medium-high. Place ham steaks on greased grill. Brush steaks with about 2 tbsp. (30 mL) remaining sauce. Cook for about 5 minutes until lightly browned. Turn. Brush with remaining sauce. Cook for 2 to 3 minutes until glazed and heated through. Serves 8.

1 serving: 228 Calories; 10.9 g Total Fat (6.2 g Mono, 1.2 g Poly, 2.9 g Sat); 51 mg Cholesterol; 9 g Carbohydrate; 0 g Fibre; 22 g Protein; 1555 mg Sodium

Pictured on page 94.

Java Ribs

Pork spareribs, cut into 3-bone portions	6 lbs.	2.7 kg
Water		
Bay leaves	2	2
Dried thyme	3/4 tsp.	4 mL
Onion salt	1/2 tsp.	2 mL
Pepper	1/2 tsp.	2 mL
COFFEE MARINADE		
Cold strong prepared coffee	1 1/4 cups	300 mL
Ketchup	1 1/4 cups	300 mL
Brown sugar, packed	2/3 cup	150 mL
Apple cider vinegar	1/2 cup	125 mL
Worcestershire sauce	4 tsp.	20 mL

The unique marinade, made with coffee, transforms tender pork ribs into a succulent feast!

Place ribs in large pot or Dutch oven. Add enough water to cover. Add next 4 ingredients. Bring to a boil on medium-high. Reduce heat to medium-low. Cover. Simmer for about 1 hour until pork is just tender. Drain and discard liquid. Cool.

Coffee Marinade: Measure all 5 ingredients into large bowl. Stir until sugar is dissolved. Makes about 3 1/2 cups (875 mL) marinade. Add ribs. Turn until coated. Cover. Let stand for 30 minutes. Drain, reserving marinade in medium saucepan. Bring reserved marinade to a boil on medium. Reduce heat to medium-low. Simmer, uncovered, for at least 5 minutes. Preheat barbecue to medium. Cook ribs on greased grill for 15 to 20 minutes, turning occasionally and brushing with reserved marinade, until glazed and heated through. Serves 8.

1 serving: 500 Calories; 26.5 g Total Fat (11.8 g Mono, 2.4 g Poly, 9.7 g Sat); 128 mg Cholesterol; 31 g Carbohydrate; 1 g Fibre; 34 g Protein; 622 mg Sodium

Pictured on pages 94/95.

Fragrant and tender—these will have everyone asking for more!

Lamb Kabobs

LEMON GINGER MARINADE

Cooking oil	1/2 cup	125 mL
Lemon juice	1/4 cup	60 mL
Ground ginger	3/4 tsp.	4 mL
Garlic powder	1/2 tsp.	2 mL
Paprika	1/2 tsp.	2 mL
Whole green cardamom, bruised (see Note)	5	5
Pepper	1/8 tsp.	0.5 mL
Lamb stew meat	1 1/2 lbs.	680 g
Medium onion, cut into 1 inch (2.5 cm) pieces	1	1
Green medium pepper, seeds and ribs removed, cut into 1 inch (2.5 cm) pieces	1	1
Bamboo skewers (8 inch, 20 cm, length), soaked in water for 10 minutes	12	12

Salt, sprinkle

Lemon Ginger Marinade: Combine first 7 ingredients in large bowl. Makes about 3/4 cup (175 mL) marinade.

Add lamb, onion and green pepper. Stir until coated. Cover. Marinate in refrigerator for 3 1/2 to 4 hours, stirring occasionally. Drain, reserving marinade in small saucepan. Bring reserved marinade to a boil on medium. Reduce heat to medium-low. Simmer, uncovered, for at least 5 minutes.

Thread lamb, onion and green pepper alternately onto skewers. Preheat barbecue to medium-high. Cook kabobs on greased grill for 15 to 20 minutes, turning occasionally and brushing with reserved marinade, until desired doneness.

Sprinkle with salt. Makes 12 kabobs.

1 kabob: 171 Calories; 12.7 g Total Fat (6.9 g Mono, 3.1 g Poly, 1.8 g Sat); 37 mg Cholesterol; 2 g Carbohydrate; trace Fibre; 12 g Protein; 32 mg Sodium

Pictured on page 99.

Wieners and sauerkraut are a natural pair.

Frankly Sauerkraut

Wieners	12	12
Prepared mustard	2 tbsp.	30 mL
Sauerkraut, drained	1 1/2 cups	375 mL
Ketchup (optional)	2 tbsp.	30 mL
Hot dog buns, split and toasted (buttered, optional)	12	12
Chopped onion, cooked if desired	1 cup	250 mL

Slice each wiener almost in half lengthwise, but not quite through to other side. Press open. Spread 1/2 tsp. (2 mL) mustard evenly on both cut sides of each wiener. Place 1 wiener, cut-side up, on each of 12 individual sheets of heavy-duty (or double layer of regular) foil. Spoon about 2 tbsp. (30 mL) sauerkraut onto each wiener. Spread evenly. Fold edges of foil to enclose. Preheat barbecue to medium. Place packets on ungreased grill. Close lid. Cook for about 5 minutes, turning once, until heated through. Remove and discard foil.

Spread 1/2 tsp. (2 mL) ketchup evenly on top half of each bun. Place 1 wiener on bottom half of each bun. Top each with onion. Cover each with top half of bun. Makes 12 hot dogs.

1 hot dog: 245 Calories; 11.2 g Total Fat (5.3 g Mono, 1.3 g Poly, 3.8 g Sat); 19 mg Cholesterol; 27 g Carbohydrate; trace Fibre; 8 g Protein; 855 mg Sodium

Pictured on page 101.

Use fine wire to secure husks to corncobs, if necessary, to keep in place for grilling.

corn in foil

Remove and discard husks and silk from corncobs. Place 1 cob on each of 6 individual sheets of heavy-duty (or double layer of regular) foil. Spread margarine on cobs. Sprinkle each with salt and pepper. Fold edges of foil to enclose. Place on ungreased grill. Close lid. Cook for about 12 minutes, turning cobs 1/4 turn every 3 minutes, until tender.

husky corn

Cook corncobs with husks and silk intact on ungreased grill for about 12 minutes, turning 1/4 turn every 3 minutes, until tender. Remove and discard husks and silk. Spread margarine on cobs. Sprinkle each with salt and pepper.

Quick Corn

Medium corncobs in husks	6	6
Hard margarine (or butter), softened	1/2 cup	125 mL
Salt, sprinkle		
Pepper, sprinkle		

Pull husks down to end of corncobs, leaving them attached to cobs. Remove and discard silk. Spread margarine evenly on cobs. Sprinkle each with salt and pepper. Bring husks back up to cover cobs. Preheat barbecue to medium. Place cobs on ungreased grill. Close lid. Cook for about 12 minutes, turning cobs 1/4 turn every 3 minutes, until tender. Remove and discard husks. Serves 6.

1 serving: 274 Calories; 17.6 g Total Fat (10.9 g Mono, 2.3 g Poly, 3.5 g Sat); 0 mg Cholesterol; 31 g Carbohydrate; 4 g Fibre; 4 g Protein; 209 mg Sodium

Pictured on page 103.

Tender, colourful vegetables and toasted bread cubes make a wonderful kabob combination.

Veggie Bread Kabobs

BALSAMIC SAUCE

Olive (or cooking) oil	1/3 cup	75 mL
Balsamic vinegar	3 tbsp.	50 mL
Sun-dried tomatoes in oil, drained	2 tbsp.	30 mL
Coarsely chopped fresh parsley (or 1 1/2 tsp., 7 mL, flakes)	2 tbsp.	30 mL
Liquid honey	1 tbsp.	15 mL
Garlic clove (or 1/4 tsp., 1 mL, powder)	1	1
Salt	1/4 tsp.	1 mL
Medium zucchini (with peel), cut into 1/2 inch (12 mm) thick slices	2	2
Fresh whole white mushrooms	20	20
Red medium peppers, seeds and ribs removed, cut into 1 inch (2.5 cm) pieces	2	2
Sourdough bread loaf, cut into 1 inch (2.5 cm) cubes	1	1
Bamboo skewers (10 inch, 25 cm, length), soaked in water for 10 minutes	10	10

Balsamic Sauce: Process first 7 ingredients in blender or food processor until smooth. Makes about 3/4 cup (175 mL) sauce.

Thread zucchini, mushrooms, red pepper and bread cubes alternately onto skewers. Place in single layer in large shallow baking dish. Brush kabobs with sauce. Cover. Let stand for 30 minutes. Preheat barbecue to medium. Cook kabobs on greased grill for about 15 minutes, turning occasionally, until bread is crisp and vegetables are tender. Makes 10 kabobs.

1 kabob: 225 Calories; 9.4 g Total Fat (6.3 g Mono, 1.1 g Poly, 1.4 g Sat); 0 mg Cholesterol; 31 g Carbohydrate; 3 g Fibre; 6 g Protein; 343 mg Sodium

Pictured on page 106.

Vegetable Skewers With Pesto Dressing

PESTO DRESSING

Fresh basil leaves	3/4 cup	175 mL
Italian salad dressing	1/4 cup	60 mL
Grated Parmesan cheese	3 tbsp.	50 mL
Pine nuts, toasted (see Note)	2 tbsp.	30 mL
Garlic clove, chopped (or 1/4 tsp., 1 mL, powder)	1	1
Salt	1/8 tsp.	0.5 mL
Pepper	1/4 tsp.	1 mL
Medium zucchini (with peel), cut into 3/4 inch (2 cm) cubes	1 – 2	1 – 2
Red medium pepper, seeds and ribs removed, cut into 1 inch (2.5 cm) pieces	1	1
Yellow medium pepper, seeds and ribs removed, cut into 1 inch (2.5 cm) pieces	1	1
Small red onion, cut into wedges	1	1
Metal skewers (10 inch, 25 cm, length), or bamboo skewers (10 inch, 25 cm, length), soaked in water for 10 minutes	6	6

Colourful vegetables glistening on the barbecue are bound to attract the attention of your guests. Make the pesto dressing ahead of time to blend flavours.

note

To toast nuts, spread evenly in ungreased shallow pan. Bake in 350°F (175°C) oven for 5 to 10 minutes, stirring or shaking often, until desired doneness.

Pesto Dressing: Process first 7 ingredients in blender or food processor until smooth. Makes about 1/2 cup (125 mL) dressing.

Put next 4 ingredients into large bowl. Toss gently. Add 1/4 cup (60 mL) dressing to vegetable mixture. Toss gently. Set remaining dressing aside.

Thread vegetables alternately onto skewers. Preheat barbecue to medium. Cook skewers on greased grill for 12 to 15 minutes, turning occasionally, until vegetables are tender-crisp. Serve with remaining dressing. Makes 6 skewers.

1 skewer with 2 tsp. (10 mL) dressing: 122 Calories; 10.1 g Total Fat (4.9 g Mono, 3.2 g Poly, 1.4 g Sat); 9 mg Cholesterol; 7 g Carbohydrate; 2 g Fibre; 3 g Protein; 278 mg Sodium

Pictured on front cover.

Photo Legend, next page
Top Left: Foiled Yams, page 109
Centre Right: Potatoes On A Stick, page 108
Bottom Left: Veggie Bread Kabobs, page 104

It's so easy to make potatoes special for summer barbecues and patio parties. Vary this recipe by using fresh herbs, such as chives or summer savory, in place of dried.

Potatoes On A Stick

Red baby potatoes (with skin), larger ones cut in half	10	10
White baby potatoes (with skin), larger ones cut in half	10	10
Water		
Olive (or cooking) oil	2 tbsp.	30 mL
Seasoned salt	1 tsp.	5 mL
Dried basil	1/2 tsp.	2 mL
Dried whole oregano	1/2 tsp.	2 mL
Dried rosemary, crushed	1/8 tsp.	0.5 mL
Pepper, sprinkle		
Metal skewers (12 inch, 30 cm, length)	4	4

Cook potatoes in water in medium saucepan until tender but still firm. Drain. Let stand until cool enough to handle.

Combine next 6 ingredients in small bowl.

Thread potatoes, alternating red and white, onto skewers, using 5 potatoes for each. Brush potatoes with olive oil mixture. Preheat barbecue to high. Place skewers on greased grill. Close lid. Cook for about 30 minutes, turning occasionally and brushing with remaining olive oil mixture, until desired doneness. Makes 4 skewers.

1 skewer: 200 Calories; 7.1 g Total Fat (5.1 g Mono, 0.7 g Poly, 1 g Sat); 0 mg Cholesterol; 31 g Carbohydrate; 3 g Fibre; 4 g Protein; 310 mg Sodium

Pictured on page 107.

Foiled Yams

Medium yams (or sweet potatoes), peeled	4	4
Hard margarine (or butter), softened	2 tbsp.	30 mL
Salt, sprinkle		
Pepper, sprinkle		

Cut 1 yam crosswise into 1/4 to 1/2 inch (6 to 12 mm) thick slices. Place slices on 1 sheet of heavy-duty (or double layer of regular) foil. Dab 1 1/2 tsp. (7 mL) margarine randomly on yam slices. Sprinkle with salt and pepper. Fold edges of foil to enclose. Repeat with remaining yams, margarine, salt and pepper, for a total of 4 packets. Preheat barbecue to medium. Place packets on ungreased grill. Close lid. Cook for 15 to 20 minutes, turning once, until yam is tender. Serves 4.

1 serving: 205 Calories; 6 g Total Fat (3.8 g Mono, 0.7 g Poly, 1.2 g Sat); 0 mg Cholesterol; 36 g Carbohydrate; 5 g Fibre; 2 g Protein; 80 mg Sodium

Pictured on page 106.

A tasty, easy-to-make side dish to add to your favourite barbecue menu.

grilled yams

Cut yams crosswise into 1/2 to 3/4 inch (12 to 20 mm) thick slices. Brush 1 side of each slice with cooking oil. Preheat barbecue to medium. Place yam slices, brushed-side down, on greased grill. Brush top sides with cooking oil. Close lid. Cook for 8 to 10 minutes per side until yam is tender. Serves 4.

foiled turnips

Cook turnips as for Foiled Yams, increasing cooking time to 20 to 25 minutes.

Creamy sauce smothers mushrooms cooked to perfection in foil packets. A terrific accompaniment for Best Pork Chops, page 92.

Mushroom Packets

Hard margarine (or butter)	2 tbsp.	30 mL
Finely chopped onion	1/2 cup	125 mL
All-purpose flour	1 tbsp.	15 mL
Chicken bouillon powder	1 tsp.	5 mL
Paprika	1/4 tsp.	1 mL
Salt	1/4 tsp.	1 mL
Pepper, sprinkle		
Sour cream	1/2 cup	125 mL
Small fresh whole white mushrooms	1 lb.	454 g

Melt margarine in medium frying pan on medium. Add onion. Cook for 5 to 10 minutes, stirring often, until softened.

Add next 5 ingredients. Heat and stir for 1 minute. Slowly add sour cream, stirring constantly, until boiling and thickened. Cool.

Divide and place mushrooms on each of 4 individual sheets of heavy-duty (or double layer of regular) foil. Divide and spoon sour cream mixture over top of each. Fold edges of foil to enclose. Preheat barbecue to medium. Place packets on ungreased grill. Close lid. Cook for 8 to 10 minutes, rotating once, until heated through. Serves 4.

1 serving: 144 Calories; 10.7 g Total Fat (5.1 g Mono, 1 g Poly, 3.9 g Sat); 12 mg Cholesterol; 10 g Carbohydrate; 2 g Fibre; 4 g Protein; 397 mg Sodium

Pictured on page 111.

These tender-crisp asparagus spears are very appetizing.

Barbecued Asparagus

Vanilla (or plain) yogurt	1/4 cup	60 mL
Lemon pepper	2 tsp.	10 mL
White vinegar	1/2 tsp.	2 mL
Cooking oil	1/2 tsp.	2 mL
Fresh asparagus, trimmed of tough ends	1 lb.	454 g

(continued on next page)

Combine first 4 ingredients in small cup.

Preheat barbecue to medium. Arrange asparagus spears crosswise in single layer on greased grill. Lightly brush asparagus with yogurt mixture. Cook for 2 minutes. Brush asparagus with yogurt mixture, gently turning spears 1/4 turn. Cook for 1 to 2 minutes. Brush and turn twice more, cooking for 1 to 2 minutes after each turn, until asparagus is glazed and tender-crisp. Serves 6.

1 serving: 29 Calories; 0.7 g Total Fat (0.3 g Mono, 0.2 g Poly, 0.2 g Sat); 1 mg Cholesterol; 5 g Carbohydrate; 1 g Fibre; 2 g Protein; 403 mg Sodium

Pictured below.

Top: Mushroom Packets, page 110
Bottom: Barbecued Asparagus, page 110

A hearty mixture of root vegetables. Roasting intensifies the natural flavour of each fresh ingredient.

Roasted Vegetable Mix

Yellow turnip (rutabaga), peeled, cut into 1 inch (2.5 cm) cubes	2 1/2 cups	625 mL
Baby carrots	36	36
Medium potatoes (with skin), quartered	5	5
Medium onions, quartered	3	3
Hard margarine (or butter)	3 tbsp.	50 mL
Olive (or cooking) oil	1 tbsp.	15 mL
Water	1 tbsp.	15 mL
Garlic cloves, minced (or 1/2 tsp., 2 mL, powder)	2	2
Dried whole oregano	1 tsp.	5 mL
Dried thyme	1 tsp.	5 mL
Dried rosemary, crushed	1 tsp.	5 mL
Seasoned salt	1 tsp.	5 mL
Pepper, sprinkle		

Place first 4 ingredients in large greased foil pan. Toss.

Melt margarine in small saucepan on low. Add remaining 8 ingredients. Stir. Drizzle over vegetable mixture. Toss until coated. Cover with foil. Preheat barbecue to high. Place pan on 1 side of ungreased grill. Turn burner under pan to low, turning opposite burner down to medium. Close lid. Cook for about 30 minutes, shaking pan occasionally, until vegetables are heated through. Remove foil. Stir. Close lid. Cook for about 30 minutes until vegetables are tender and starting to brown. Serves 6.

1 serving: 240 Calories; 8.6 g Total Fat (5.5 g Mono, 1 g Poly, 1.6 g Sat); 0 mg Cholesterol; 38 g Carbohydrate; 6 g Fibre; 5 g Protein; 343 mg Sodium

Pictured on page 113.

Fresh, glazed peaches with visible grill marks. Delicious served with grilled croissants and ice cream.

Balsamic Peaches

Fresh peaches (with skin), cut in half and pits removed (see Note)	6	6
Balsamic vinegar	1/3 cup	75 mL
Liquid honey, warmed	1/4 cup	60 mL
Croissants, cut in half horizontally	3	3
Hard margarine (or butter), melted	2 tbsp.	30 mL
Vanilla ice cream	1 1/2 cups	375 mL
Fresh raspberries	1/2 cup	125 mL

Put peaches into large non-metal bowl. Add vinegar. Toss gently. Cover. Chill for 1 hour, stirring occasionally. Drain and discard liquid.

Preheat barbecue to medium. Cook peaches on greased grill for about 5 minutes per side, brushing with honey, until browned and grill marks appear.

Brush cut sides of croissants with margarine. Cook croissants on greased grill for about 2 minutes per side until crisp and grill marks appear.

Place 1 croissant half, 2 peach halves and 1/4 cup (60 mL) ice cream (about 1 scoop) on each of 6 individual plates.

Sprinkle raspberries over top of each. Serves 6.

1 serving: 338 Calories; 14.9 g Total Fat (5.6 g Mono, 1 g Poly, 7.1 g Sat); 40 mg Cholesterol; 50 g Carbohydrate; 3 g Fibre; 5 g Protein; 323 mg Sodium

Pictured on page 115.

Lemon zest adds a nice balance to sweet grilled cake topped with strawberries and cream. Looks good—tastes heavenly!

Grilled Cake And Strawberries

Maple (or maple-flavoured) syrup	1/2 cup	125 mL
Orange juice	1/3 cup	75 mL
Hard margarine (or butter), melted	2 tbsp.	30 mL
Grated lemon zest	1 tsp.	5 mL
Frozen pound cake, thawed	10 1/2 oz.	298 g
STRAWBERRY TOPPING		
Lemon spread	1/2 cup	125 mL
Whipping cream (or half-and-half cream)	2 tbsp.	30 mL
Halved (or quartered, if large) fresh strawberries	3 cups	750 mL

Combine first 4 ingredients in small bowl.

Remove and discard crust from cake. Cut cake crosswise into 6 equal slices. Cut each slice in half diagonally, for a total of 12 pieces. Dip both sides of each piece into maple syrup mixture. Preheat barbecue to medium. Cook cake on greased grill for about 3 minutes per side until grill marks appear. Place 2 cake slices on each of 6 individual plates.

Strawberry Topping: Heat and stir lemon spread and whipping cream in small saucepan on medium for about 3 minutes until lemon spread is melted. Remove from heat. Let stand for 5 minutes.

Put strawberries into medium bowl. Drizzle with lemon spread mixture. Toss gently. Makes about 3 cups (750 mL) topping. Spoon about 1/2 cup (125 mL) topping over each cake serving. Serves 6.

1 serving: 376 Calories; 15.2 g Total Fat (8.1 g Mono, 1.7 g Poly, 4.4 g Sat); 36 mg Cholesterol; 58 g Carbohydrate; 2 g Fibre; 4 g Protein; 319 mg Sodium

Pictured on page 117 and on back cover.

Top: Chocolate Pizza, page 118
Bottom: Grilled Cake And Strawberries, above

Decadence cloaked in a chocolate cookie crust and creamy, hot fudge topping. Almond liqueur mellows the sweetness of the chocolate.

note

To toast almonds, spread evenly in ungreased shallow pan. Bake in 350°F (175°C) oven for 5 to 10 minutes, stirring or shaking often, until desired doneness.

Chocolate Pizza

Tube of refrigerator chocolate cookie dough	16 oz.	454 g
Granulated sugar	1 tbsp.	15 mL
Ricotta cheese	2 cups	500 mL
Hot fudge ice cream topping	1/4 – 1/3 cup	60 – 75 mL
Sour cream	1/4 cup	60 mL
Almond-flavoured liqueur (such as Amaretto)	3 tbsp.	50 mL
Sliced almonds, toasted (see Note)	1/3 cup	75 mL
Hot fudge ice cream topping	2 – 3 tbsp.	30 – 50 mL

Press cookie dough evenly in ungreased 12 inch (30 cm) pizza pan. Sprinkle with sugar. Preheat barbecue to high. Place pan on 1 side of ungreased grill. Turn off burner under pan, turning opposite burner down to medium. Close lid. Cook for about 10 minutes until edge of cookie is just set. Cool.

Process next 4 ingredients in blender or food processor until smooth. Spread cheese mixture evenly on crust.

Sprinkle with almonds. Drizzle with second amount of ice cream topping. Cuts into 12 wedges.

1 wedge: 327 Calories; 17.2 g Total Fat (7.1 g Mono, 1.7 g Poly, 7.5 g Sat); 34 mg Cholesterol; 35 g Carbohydrate; trace Fibre; 8 g Protein; 133 mg Sodium

Pictured on page 117 and on back cover.

Bananas Caramel

Hard margarine (or butter)	1/2 cup	125 mL
Brown sugar, packed	1/2 cup	125 mL
Sweetened condensed milk	1/2 cup	125 mL
Corn syrup	2 tbsp.	30 mL
Medium bananas, halved lengthwise	4	4
Chopped pecans (or walnuts)	1/3 cup	75 mL

Combine first 4 ingredients in small heavy saucepan. Bring to a boil on medium. Boil, stirring constantly, for 5 minutes. Remove from heat.

Place 2 banana halves on each of 4 individual sheets of heavy-duty (or double layer of regular) foil. Divide and spoon brown sugar mixture evenly over top of each. Fold edges of foil to enclose. Preheat barbecue to medium. Place packets on ungreased grill. Close lid. Cook for 8 to 10 minutes, without turning, until heated through. Transfer bananas to 4 individual plates. Drizzle sauce from foil over each.

Sprinkle each with pecans. Serves 4.

1 serving: 658 Calories; 35.2 g Total Fat (21.1 g Mono, 4.3 g Poly, 7.9 g Sat); 14 mg Cholesterol; 87 g Carbohydrate; 3 g Fibre; 5 g Protein; 359 mg Sodium

Pictured on page 120.

A fantastic dessert that's quick and easy to make for a bunch! Each grilled bite becomes even sweeter with rich caramel sauce.

variation

Cut bananas into 1/2 inch (12 mm) thick slices. Prepare and cook as directed. Serve in 4 individual dessert bowls.

Pictured on page 120.

Photo Legend, next page

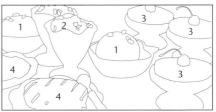

1. Grilled Apples, page 122
2. Bananas Caramel, above
3. Barbecued Grapefruit, page 123
4. Grilled Spiced Pineapple, page 122

A simple yet elegant dessert, delicious hot off the grill or made ahead of time and served cold.

note

Omit fresh pineapple slices. Used 12 canned pineapple slices, drained. Cook slices on greased grill for 1 to 2 minutes per side until grill marks appear. Serve with Ricotta Sauce.

Grilled Spiced Pineapple

Maple (or maple-flavoured) syrup	1/2 cup	125 mL
Brandy (or 1/2 tsp., 2 mL, brandy flavouring)	2 tbsp.	30 mL
Ground cinnamon	1/2 tsp.	2 mL
Ground ginger	1/2 tsp.	2 mL
Pepper	1/4 tsp.	1 mL
Slices of fresh pineapple (about 1/2 inch, 12 mm, thick), see Note	6	6
RICOTTA SAUCE		
Ricotta cheese	1 cup	250 mL
Low-fat vanilla yogurt	1/2 cup	125 mL

Combine first 5 ingredients in small bowl. Reserve 2 tbsp. (30 mL) in small cup.

Brush remaining maple syrup mixture evenly over both sides of each pineapple slice. Preheat barbecue to medium. Cook pineapple slices on greased grill for 3 to 5 minutes per side until grill marks appear. Transfer pineapple slices to 6 individual plates.

Ricotta Sauce: Combine ricotta cheese, yogurt and reserved maple syrup mixture in medium bowl. Makes about 1 1/2 cups (375 mL) sauce. Spoon about 1/4 cup (60 mL) sauce into centre of each pineapple slice. Serves 6.

1 serving: 190 Calories; 5.8 g Total Fat (1.6 g Mono, 0.2 g Poly, 3.6 g Sat); 22 mg Cholesterol; 27 g Carbohydrate; 1 g Fibre; 6 g Protein; 55 mg Sodium

Pictured on page 120.

An easy recipe to double or triple for a crowd. Good with or without the raisins. When these are unwrapped, the aroma will have everyone desiring dessert!

Grilled Apples

Medium cooking apples (such as McIntosh), with peel, cores removed	4	4
Brown sugar, packed	1/2 cup	125 mL
Raisins (or currants)	2 tbsp.	30 mL
Ground cinnamon	1/8 tsp.	0.5 mL
Hard margarine (or butter), softened	2 tsp.	10 mL

(continued on next page)

Place 1 apple on each of 4 individual sheets of heavy-duty (or double layer of regular) foil.

Combine brown sugar, raisins and cinnamon in small bowl. Divide and spoon brown sugar mixture into centre of each apple.

Place 1/2 tsp. (2 mL) margarine on top of each. Fold edges of foil to enclose. Preheat barbecue to medium. Place packets on ungreased grill. Close lid. Cook for 15 to 20 minutes, turning occasionally, until apples are softened. Transfer apples to 4 individual plates. Drizzle sauce from foil over each. Serves 4.

1 serving: 222 Calories; 2.5 g Total Fat (1.3 g Mono, 0.3 g Poly, 0.5 g Sat); 0 mg Cholesterol; 53 g Carbohydrate; 3 g Fibre; 0 g Protein; 35 mg Sodium

Pictured on pages 120/121.

Barbecued Grapefruit

Pink medium grapefruit	3	3
Brown sugar, packed	6 tbsp.	100 mL
Dry sherry	6 tbsp.	100 mL
Maraschino cherries, for garnish	6	6

An absolute treat for breakfast or brunch. Use more brown sugar and sherry to make more juices for drizzling if desired. Simply scrumptious!

Cut grapefruit in half crosswise. Remove and discard seeds. Run knife along membranes to loosen fruit segments. Place 1 grapefruit half, cut-side up, on each of 6 individual sheets of heavy-duty (or double layer of regular) foil. Sprinkle each grapefruit half with 1 tbsp. (15 mL) brown sugar and 1 tbsp. (15 mL) sherry. Fold edges of foil to enclose. Preheat barbecue to medium. Place packets on ungreased grill. Close lid. Cook for 10 to 12 minutes until heated through. Transfer grapefruit halves to 6 individual plates.

Garnish each with 1 maraschino cherry. Drizzle with any juices left in foil. Serves 6.

1 serving: 102 Calories; 0.1 g Total Fat (0 g Mono, 0 g Poly, 0 g Sat); 0 mg Cholesterol; 24 g Carbohydrate; 2 g Fibre; 1 g Protein; 6 mg Sodium

Pictured on page 121.

Throughout this book measurements are given in Conventional and Metric measure. To compensate for differences between the two measurements due to rounding, a full metric measure is not always used. The cup used is the standard 8 fluid ounce. Temperature is given in degrees Fahrenheit and Celsius. Baking pan measurements are in inches and centimetres as well as quarts and litres. An exact metric conversion is given on this page as well as the working equivalent (Metric Standard Measure).

Pans

Conventional – Inches	Metric – Centimetres
8 × 8 inch	20 × 20 cm
9 × 9 inch	22 × 22 cm
9 × 13 inch	22 × 33 cm
10 × 15 inch	25 × 38 cm
11 × 17 inch	28 × 43 cm
8 × 2 inch round	20 × 5 cm
9 × 2 inch round	22 × 5 cm
10 × 4 1/2 inch tube	25 × 11 cm
8 × 4 × 3 inch loaf	20 × 10 × 7.5 cm
9 × 5 × 3 inch loaf	22 × 12.5 × 7.5 cm

Oven Temperatures

Fahrenheit (°F)	Celsius (°C)	Fahrenheit (°F)	Celsius (°C)
175°	80°	350°	175°
200°	95°	375°	190°
225°	110°	400°	205°
250°	120°	425°	220°
275°	140°	450°	230°
300°	150°	475°	240°
325°	160°	500°	260°

Spoons

Conventional Measure	Metric Exact Conversion Millilitre (mL)	Metric Standard Measure Millilitre (mL)
1/8 teaspoon (tsp.)	0.6 mL	0.5 mL
1/4 teaspoon (tsp.)	1.2 mL	1 mL
1/2 teaspoon (tsp.)	2.4 mL	2 mL
1 teaspoon (tsp.)	4.7 mL	5 mL
2 teaspoons (tsp.)	9.4 mL	10 mL
1 tablespoon (tbsp.)	14.2 mL	15 mL

Cups

1/4 cup (4 tbsp.)	56.8 mL	60 mL
1/3 cup (5 1/3 tbsp.)	75.6 mL	75 mL
1/2 cup (8 tbsp.)	113.7 mL	125 mL
2/3 cup (10 2/3 tbsp.)	151.2 mL	150 mL
3/4 cup (12 tbsp.)	170.5 mL	175 mL
1 cup (16 tbsp.)	227.3 mL	250 mL
4 1/2 cups	1022.9 mL	1000 mL (1 L)

Dry Measurements

Conventional Measure Ounces (oz.)	Metric Exact Conversion Grams (g)	Metric Standard Measure Grams (g)
1 oz.	28.3 g	28 g
2 oz.	56.7 g	57 g
3 oz.	85.0 g	85 g
4 oz.	113.4 g	125 g
5 oz.	141.7 g	140 g
6 oz.	170.1 g	170 g
7 oz.	198.4 g	200 g
8 oz.	226.8 g	250 g
16 oz.	453.6 g	500 g
32 oz.	907.2 g	1000 g (1 kg)

Casseroles

Canada & Britain

Standard Size Casserole	Exact Metric Measure
1 qt. (5 cups)	1.13 L
1 1/2 qts. (7 1/2 cups)	1.69 L
2 qts. (10 cups)	2.25 L
2 1/2 qts. (12 1/2 cups)	2.81 L
3 qts. (15 cups)	3.38 L
4 qts. (20 cups)	4.5 L
5 qts. (25 cups)	5.63 L

United States

Standard Size Casserole	Exact Metric Measure
1 qt. (4 cups)	900 mL
1 1/2 qts. (6 cups)	1.35 L
2 qts. (8 cups)	1.8 L
2 1/2 qts. (10 cups)	2.25 L
3 qts. (12 cups)	2.7 L
4 qts. (16 cups)	3.6 L
5 qts. (20 cups)	4.5 L

most loved recipe collection most loved recipe collection most loved recipe collection
loved recipe collection most loved recipe collection most loved recipe collection most
ection most loved recipe collection most loved recipe collection most loved recipe colle
most loved recipe collection most loved recipe collection most loved recipe collection
tion most loved recipe collection most loved recipe collection most loved recipe collec
most loved recipe collection most loved recipe collection most loved recipe collection
e collection most loved recipe collection most loved recipe collection most loved recip
ection most loved recipe collection most loved recipe collection most loved recipe colle
most loved recipe collection most loved recipe collection most loved recipe collection
loved recipe collection most loved recipe collection most loved recipe collection most
ection most loved recipe collection most loved recipe collection most loved recipe colle
most loved recipe collection most loved recipe collection most loved recipe collection
tion most loved recipe collection most loved recipe collection most loved recipe collec
most loved recipe collection most loved recipe collection most loved recipe collection
e collection most loved recipe collection most loved recipe collection most loved recip
ection most loved recipe collection most loved recipe collection most loved recipe colle
most loved recipe collection most loved recipe collection most loved recipe collection
loved recipe collection most loved recipe collection most loved recipe collection most
ection most loved recipe collection most loved recipe collection most loved recipe colle
most loved recipe collection most loved recipe collection most loved recipe collection
tion most loved recipe collection most loved recipe collection most loved recipe collec
most loved recipe collection most loved recipe collection most loved recipe collection
e collection most loved recipe collection most loved recipe collection most loved recip
ection most loved recipe collection most loved recipe collection most loved recipe colle
most loved recipe collection most loved recipe collection most loved recipe collection
loved recipe collection most loved recipe collection most loved recipe collection most
ection most loved recipe collection most loved recipe collection most loved recipe colle
most loved recipe collection most loved recipe collection most loved recipe collection
tion most loved recipe collection most loved recipe collection most loved recipe collec
most loved recipe collection most loved recipe collection most loved recipe collection
pe collection most loved recipe collection most loved recipe collection most loved recip